GUIDE TO
INSPECTING
YOUR HOME

Real Estate
Education Company
a division of Dearborn Financial Publishing, Inc.

Acquisitions Editor: Christine E. Litavsky
Managing Editor: Jack Kiburz
Interior Design: Lucy Jenkins
Cover Design: ST & Associates

Published by Real Estate Education Company®,
a division of Dearborn Financial Publishing, Inc.®

Library of Congress Cataloging-in-Publication Data

CENTURY 21® guide to inspecting your home / CENTURY 21®.
   p. cm.
  Includes index.
  ISBN 0-7931-1782-8 (paper)
  1. Dwellings—Inspection—Amateurs' manuals. 2. House buying—
Amateurs' manuals. I. CENTURY 21® (Firm)
TH4817.5.C442 1996
643'.12—dc20   95-50803
                                     CIP

CONTENTS

PREFACE

Home ownership—the American dream! For millions of families, their home is not only their "castle" but their single largest investment—and the foundation of their financial stability.

But how do you make sure that dream home does not turn into a nightmare—full of unexpected repairs, unanticipated expenses and unsuitable qualities that cramp your lifestyle and plague your pocketbook for years to come?

The answers are all here in the *CENTURY 21® Guide to Inspecting Your Home.* Step-by-step, this comprehensive manual shows you what to look for, what to think about and what to ask in viewing a prospective residence. It will help you weigh issues ranging from lifestyle to location, as well as matters of value, maintenance and structural integrity. You will also learn our top brokers' tricks of the trade to ensure that what you see is indeed what you get.

This book is packed with money-saving tips (50 in all), collected from our top professionals and designed to help you stretch your homebuying dollars. To address lingering doubts or concerns, each chapter ends with answers to the questions most commonly asked by homebuyers like you.

It's what you'd expect from the company that symbolizes home ownership—and whose brokers and associates in your community stand at the ready to help you put these strategies into action.

All of us in the *CENTURY 21®* System—*the* source for homeowner information and services—wish you the best in pursuing your dream of home ownership and many years of happy living in your "castle."

CHAPTER 1

Understanding the Need for a Home Inspection

Buying or selling a house is no time for playing hunches. There's too much at stake, both in money and in peace of mind.

If you're close to buying a home, call in an inspector before you've reached a final agreement to purchase the property. Ten years ago, home inspection—a visual examination of the systems that make up a house, from foundation to roof—was a minor part of real estate transactions. Today, however, as a result of consumer protection measures, a significant and growing percentage of existing houses—and even some new houses—are inspected at the time of sale. In fact, a growing number of banks now require a professional home inspection as an integral part of the purchase procedure.

The American Society of Home Inspectors estimates that about half of all homes on the resale market have at least one significant defect, and nearly all homes need some maintenance and repair work.

A professional inspection can help the seller, too. A presale inspection can alert the seller to problems that could complicate a potential sale. Correcting these problems early not only makes the property more desirable, but it also simplifies the negotiation process when the time comes for the buyer's prepurchase home inspection.

The *CENTURY 21® Guide to Inspecting Your Home* explains how to conduct preliminary home inspections on your own. The inspection process involves neighborhood and site analysis as well as examining the house itself from foundation to roof. The intent here is not to do away with professional home inspectors. We firmly believe they are a necessary ingredient in the purchasing process. But as a buyer, no doubt you will look at many houses before you narrow your choices down to one or two. And with professional inspectors charging up to $400 per inspection, it would be financially imprudent for you to have each house you are considering inspected by an expert. Your ability to spot good points and special features as well as defects in a house will enable you to sort through your selection of homes and delay calling in the professional inspector for the one house that seems most promising.

Sellers, on the other hand, need a home inspection for different reasons. With the growing concern about consumer protection, the courts have been modifying the *caveat emptor* principle—let the buyer beware—by placing more responsibility on the seller.

As a result, buyers today are far more likely than ever before to hold sellers responsible for problems discovered after the contract is signed. So, it just makes good sense for the seller to be up front with the buyer about known problems or areas in need of repair and even potential troublespots.

Disclosure

As a result of recent court cases and new state laws, sellers are increasingly being asked to disclose known defects right from the start. Sellers have long been liable for misrepresentations about major defects, including the withholding of information about hidden problems. And most states hold sellers responsible for any major defect they knew about or could reasonably have known about.

Under most state laws, sellers must tell buyers about hidden flaws if there is something that would change the buyer's assessment of the property's value—for example, a bad septic system, a leaky basement or a cracked foundation.

Adding to the burden on sellers are concerns over radon, lead, asbestos and other health threats. While no state requires sellers to test for such substances, the new laws generally require them to spell out what they know or don't know.

The Professional Home Inspector

Once you've found the right house and decide you want to buy it, consider hiring a professional home inspector before you sign on the dotted line. An expert can pinpoint problems that neophyte buyers might overlook, and a home inspection is essential if buyers want to know what they are getting. A defect or dangerous condition deliberately concealed by the seller or by the real estate agent could be the basis for legal action.

The inspection should cover foundations and basement slabs, roofing, walls, ceilings, floors, windows and doors. An inspector will determine whether main structural components are sound, free from rot or insect damage, and strong enough to support the weight of the house.

The home inspector will check out all exposed water and waste pipes, faucets, drainage, water heaters and connections to appliances. The inspector will also evaluate the overall condition of the electrical system to see that it's adequate for your current and future needs.

Grounding connections and exposed wiring will be tested for overload protection, and heating and cooling systems will be tested for efficiency.

Home inspectors look for termite damage, but some are not licensed to evaluate whether termites are present. A termite report, usually required by a financial institution before it will issue a mortgage, should come from a licensed pest-control company.

A typical home inspection generally does not include looking for environmental hazards—the presence of contaminants in water, radon gas, leaking underground storage tanks, asbestos, lead paint or urea formaldehyde foam insulation, to name a few. An environmental assessment of the property must be made by someone trained to identify and test for potential environmental hazards.

A home inspection typically costs between $200 and $400 for an evaluation of the mechanical and structural components of a home and, if needed, another $200 to $300 for a formal environmental assessment.

☞ **Money-$aving Tip #1** *Professional home inspectors can save buyers thousands of dollars if faults are found, or at the very least give buyers peace of mind to know that they are making a sound purchase.*

Home Inspection as a Negotiating Tool

As a buyer, another benefit of having a professional home inspection is that it gives you financial leverage. You can always renegotiate the price downward if any major problem you think the seller should pay for has been found. Assume, for example, that you make an offer on a home with the stipulation that the sale is contingent on your approval of a home inspection, and the offer is accepted. Now suppose the inspector finds that the roof is nearing the end of its useful life and, in his opinion, will need to be replaced shortly—even though there are no visible signs of leakage. As the buyer, you have the option of (1) calling off the deal or (2) asking the seller to either replace the roof or credit you for the replacement cost. If the seller won't pay for the whole thing, maybe he will split the cost of a new roof with you. The point is, the home inspection can be used as a negotiating tool.

☞ **Money-$aving Tip #2** *Use evident problems as bargaining chips in your deal.*

What's the House Really Worth?

You've found the right house and you want to buy it. Starting now, every signal you send the seller, either directly or through the seller's agent, is part of the bargaining process, so be careful what you say and do within earshot of either.

You know what you can afford to pay. Now you need to decide what you are willing to pay for this particular house. While emotional attachment can make a house a home, the actual value of a house depends on many factors. These include the neighborhood in which the house is located, the condition of the house, current market conditions, interest rates and the length of time the house has been for sale.

☞ **Money-$aving Tip #3** *Pay attention to the original listing date of the homes you inspect. Sellers tend to be more flexible on the price the longer a house is on the market.*

Who is valuing it and why also affect the worth of a home. Homebuyers, homesellers, mortgage lenders, insurance companies and tax authorities all have different points of view about the value of a home.

How can you determine the actual value of a home? First, your real estate professional can give you a good estimate of the home's value by doing a competitive market analysis. This means analyzing housing demands in the neighborhood, recent sales of similar properties and the availability of financing. Having an appraisal done by a professional appraiser is another way. This opinion or estimate of value is not a statement of fact. As a result, it might be subject to honest dispute. Nevertheless, an appraisal by an experienced professional comes as close to an objective evaluation as you can get. And, financial institutions insist on an appraisal to determine the amount of money they will lend to a credit applicant.

Home Warranties

Since home warranty protection was introduced in the early 1970s, it has become increasingly popular among homeowners. Home warranty protection plans cover repair and replacement costs on most major home systems and built-in appliances, including heating and cooling systems, electrical and plumbing systems, duct work, water heaters, swimming pools and much more.

☞ **Money-$aving Tip #4** *The last thing a prospective new homeowner wants to worry about is spending cash to cover a major repair expense. Make sure you are dealing* *with an agent who can offer you warranty protection on your new home.*

How *the Agent Can Help*

When you decide to move, whether it's around the corner, across town or across the country, you have specific needs. You may relocate to take a new job, get a larger home for a growing family, or you may just wish to live in a different house. Whatever the motivation, there are many factors to consider, because buying a home is a major investment.

Professional real estate brokers or agents can assist you in many ways; for example, they can

- help you determine exactly what you need in a new home;
- help you select houses to tour;
- make appointments to see those homes;
- transport you to the homes you're touring;
- help you evaluate those homes;
- get answers to your questions by acting as an intermediary between you and the listing agent or seller;
- have the seller fully disclose in writing all known defects in the home;
- offer both buyer and seller a home warranty plan;
- find a qualified home inspector in the area;
- estimate the value of homes you are interested in; and more.

Keep this in mind, however: Although they probably spend more time with buyers, most brokers and agents ultimately work for sellers. It is the seller who pays for the agent's services.

Commonly Asked Questions

Q. What's an inspection clause?

A. A stipulation in an offer-to-purchase that makes the contract contingent on the findings of a professional home inspector.

Q. What's a home warranty plan?

A. A policy purchased by a seller or buyer as insurance against unexpected home repair costs.

Q. What is meant by fair market value?

A. The most probable price an informed buyer will pay for real estate, assuming normal market conditions.

Q. What is meant by competitive market analysis (CMA)?

A. A comparison of the prices of recently sold homes that are similar to a listing seller's home in terms of location, style and amenities.

Q. Is it the job of the professional home inspector to tell the buyer or seller whether he thinks the house is worth its asking price?

A. No. The inspector's job is to make the buyer or seller aware of repairs that are recommended or necessary—not how much the house is worth. The examination includes a detailed written report covering the condition of the home's roofing, walls, ceilings, floors, windows, doors, foundation, basement slab and electromechanical systems.

CHAPTER 2

Choosing the Best Neighborhood

Comparing neighborhoods is probably the most important step a prospective buyer can take before purchasing a home in a new community. There seems to be an old saying for every event, and buying a home is no exception. "You're not buying a home, you're buying a neighborhood" certainly sums up the number one consideration for many buyers. And understandably so. You can change the exterior or interior, but how often do you move a house?

You need to evaluate many factors before "buying a neighborhood." After all, you're going to live there, so you'll want to be sure that it offers the right living environment for your family's lifestyle. At the same time, it's just as important to view your home as an investment whose future value will be greatly influenced by the neighborhood's evolution. Your dream house could turn into a bad dream if a factory springs up across the way or a superhighway bores through your backyard.

☞ **Money-$aving Tip #5** *Location has a direct effect on the market value of a property and will greatly influence your enjoyment of the house you select.*

A typical neighborhood goes through a cycle of changes in its life: *growth, stability, decline* and *revitalization.* Residential property values tend to increase during the period in which an area is first developed. When few vacant housing sites remain, the houses in the neighborhood generally reach stability at their highest value and prices will rarely fluctuate downward. As the years go by, however, and the effects of property deterioration become visible, the area will usually decline in both value and desirability. The process of decline can be accelerated by the availability of new housing nearby, successive ownership by lower-income residents who may not be able to afford the increasing maintenance costs of older homes, and conversion of some properties to rental units, which may not be properly maintained. As properties decrease in value, some may even be put to a different use, such as light industry, which in turn further decreases the attractiveness of the surrounding neighborhood for residential use. Or, if a development is being filled in with lower-cost housing, there's a good chance things are on the decline. The life cycle is not always downward, however. It may begin an upswing because of revitalization if demand increases and provides the economic stimulus needed for neighborhood renovation.

☞ **Money-$aving Tip #6** *Stay away from neighborhoods that are in decline. A period of decline begins when a neighborhood can no longer compete with comparable neighborhoods. During this period, prices may fall to attract buyers and "For Sale" signs appear more frequently.*

Evaluating the Neighborhood

A neighborhood not only affects the market value of your home, it shapes the way you live. Where will your children go to school? How long will it take you to get to work? Does the area have a low crime rate? The neighborhood affects dozens of other everyday matters. It may ultimately make more difference to your family than the house itself.

Without even talking to anyone you can tell exactly how the people in a neighborhood feel about their homes. The total visual impression is a true indicator of the community's personality. Pride is reflected in the decorative features, fresh paint, flowers, nice landscaping—the "caring" of loving owners. Older neighborhoods that have been well maintained are likely to remain that way. Homeowners are likely to stay in these areas and continue protecting their investments.

Indifference gives the impression of premature oldness to the neighborhood. When several homes appear neglected in what is otherwise a well-kept neighborhood, it may be an early sign that those homeowners are either financially hard pressed or just plain don't care. If that situation continues, within a few years the property values in that area could level off or begin to decline.

You'll also want to make sure that the home you are interested in is in the same general price range as surrounding homes. The biggest, most expensive home on the block will not have the same resale value in a moderately priced neighborhood as it would if it were located in a neighborhood of comparably or higher-priced homes. As a general rule of thumb, appraisers and mortgage lenders have found that the resale value of a relatively inexpensive home in a good area will be pulled up by the higher-priced homes, while the large, expensive home will be pulled down by surrounding lower-priced homes.

Corner lots are sometimes preferred because they usually are larger. But corner lots have more traffic to contend with, including the two- and four-legged pedestrians who believe in taking the shortest distance between two points, right across your lawn.

Try to imagine yourself living in the neighborhood. Will your sense of individuality be offended if every house has been built from the same blueprint? Does a small backyard matter? Will parking be a problem for you or your guests? Is it important to you to have better access to services and deliveries?

Talk to the Neighbors

If you get serious about a home, there is nothing wrong with knocking on a few of your prospective neighbors' doors. Introduce yourself and tell them why you are there. Find out if they own the home. The responsibility for maintaining a house lies with the owner. Renters usually depend on their landlord for major upkeep. Even if the property is well kept today, the owner's willingness or financial ability to maintain his investment could change.

Discovering common interests with neighbors is always a plus. Sharing activities is an excellent way to get acquainted and feel like you are part of the neighborhood. You may be lucky that day and find some people who will not only tell you about good things in the area but will also open up about the drawbacks or current topics of dissent.

If you have children, ask about the ages and number of children in the neighborhood. Answers here will tell you if your children will have playmates nearby. Ask about the social life of the neighborhood. Is the neighborhood's age mix balanced or is one age group more prevalent? A young, growing family, for example, may not want to live in an area where most of the people are nearing retirement age, or vice versa.

How Far Is the Outside World?

When you're evaluating neighborhoods, check the distance to the nearest police station and fire department. You'll also want easy access to shopping, schools, churches, libraries, recreation areas, medical facilities, banks, the post office and public transportation.

A quick drive around the area will give you a fair picture of what is and is not within walking distance of homes in the area.

Is your job across town? An hour's commuting time each way may be more than you can handle—or will want to. If you will have to commute, get up early one morning and make the trip from the area you are considering—by car, train or bus. See what it's like. You may have a totally different view of things by the end of the day.

Quality of Schools

If you have children, the quality of schools is important. A few visits and phone calls can help you separate rumors and opinions from facts. The local school district can provide figures on class size, achievement test scores and dollars spent per student. If you don't have children, you may prefer a community where education is not a big budget item.

The Importance of Essential Services

A utility company can truthfully claim that the best compliment is to be taken for granted. It is easy to take running water, natural gas, police and fire protection, sewer systems, garbage collection, maintained roadways and snow removal for granted, especially if you are presently living in an area where these services are provided.

Don't take anything for granted. Check into the availability and quality of these services. For example, if the sewers are already in, you will want to know if they are still adequate for the area. Have there been any problems with sewers backing up in basements? Have heavy rains caused repeated flooding or severe run-off conditions that might impair the foundation of the house?

You will also want to ask about the water system. This is something everybody takes for granted in the city. But is the water safe? Although the Environmental Protection Agency (EPA) says that every state's water supply contains some contaminants, most are kept at safe levels.

In some suburbs or rural areas, the house may be served by a well. How deep is it? Has it ever been known to go dry? How old is the pump? It might be helpful if you suddenly got thirsty and asked for a drink of water. Most well water is delicious, but once in a while you'll find a well with minerals that can do strange things to the water supply.

Is fire protection provided by a full-time or volunteer department? While volunteers have demonstrated exceptional skill in fighting fires, a paid fire department is usually better equipped and more responsive to alarms. Insurance companies usually set lower rates for fire insurance in areas that have paid fire departments.

In many semirural and some suburban areas, homeowners have the responsibility of maintaining their own septic tank, if no sewers are provided. Septic tanks need pumping out periodically. In many areas, garbage pickup is included in your taxes. If, however, a private collection service must be employed, you will need to budget for these services.

Watch for Growth Patterns

The importance of a home's location cannot be stressed enough. As stated earlier, you will probably want to be close to main roads, mass transit, good schools and shopping centers as well as be removed from major commercial sites and airports.

In addition, you'll want to find a location where real estate values are rising or are likely to rise, in case you decide to sell the house in a few years.

One of the easiest methods of estimating resale value is to review the community's growth pattern and tax history. Growth can be checked by contacting the local zoning board and asking for building permit statistics for the past several years and the year to date. Huge numbers of permits can be translated into rapid growth. Some communities seem to be able to handle instant growth better than others. Find out if any tax increases, special assessments or bond issues are on the horizon for sewage treatment plants, sewers or sidewalks. Rapidly growing areas develop ravenous appetites for new schools, too.

One of the arguments frequently heard against buying in a new area way out in the suburbs is that you will have to pay the taxes for the new schools and services. While that may be true, it doesn't necessarily mean that you should not buy the house. You usually get more house for less money when you buy in a newly developed area. You are part of the community from the beginning and have a voice in its future. If the city is growing in that direction, it won't be long before your location is considered close in and very desirable. Your property values will probably go up faster. Even with higher taxes, you may be ahead.

On the other hand, built-up areas in the city or close-in suburbs are known quantities. They have built their schools, put in their sewers and sidewalks. Their tax rate has leveled off and chances are that property values are more stable, too.

Obviously there are advantages and disadvantages to both kinds of areas. You may want to explore several areas before you decide.

How Will Zoning Affect You?

Most local ordinances specify the minimum size home you can construct on a particular lot. They also specify how close you can build to the street and adjacent property lines. Many communities have restrictive covenants that regulate the size of the house and the materials used to build it. Some even restrict architectural styles and color selections. Like codes and zoning laws, restrictive covenants are public records.

By regulating what can and cannot be built, residential neighborhoods are protected against unwanted or poorly located commercial developments. Carefully zoned areas tend to hold their property values. This can be important when it comes time to sell.

If you have any notions of expanding or converting parts of a prospective house for business purposes, zoning laws could cut these plans short. A doctor who may want to add a wing for an office may be unable to do so. A beautician who wants a salon in her home may have to look for another location.

The zoning classification of nearby undeveloped land is important, too. Today's empty field could be tomorrow's school, shopping center or parking lot. You could be the cautious person who wisely bought a house on a quiet street in a beautiful neighborhood when transferred to a new city. A year later, plans were announced for an interstate highway that would go through the meadow behind your house.

☞ **Money-$aving Tip #7** *Effective zoning laws provide protection against adverse influences that can cause property values in a neighborhood to decline.*

Environmental Concerns

During all this legwork in the neighborhood, stop and take a deep breath. Is the air clean? Do wafts of dirty, smelly stuff drift over the area at certain times of the day? Smog problems are worse in some areas than others.

The presence of environmental conditions such as smoke, fog, noxious fumes, and proximity to toxic waste dumps and old landfills not only threatens the health of neighborhood residents, but it also can have a significant negative effect on the value and marketability of property in the area.

Now that you have stopped to inhale, listen, too. How noisy is the area? Can you hear the distant drone of cars on a freeway or trucks grinding around an interchange? Is there a factory or airport nearby? Noise doesn't even have to be nearby to be irritating. If the wind patterns are right, sound can carry for miles. And it takes a long time to get used to whistles blowing every hour. But for many people the soft melodious chiming of a church bell is a soothing sound.

☞ **Money-$aving Tip #8** *Automobile and truck traffic are the most common sources of noise pollution.*

Traffic Patterns

Through traffic on residential streets presents a safety hazard, creates noise and stirs up dust. If you have small children, cars racing up and down streets may give you an advanced case of nerves.

Although many existing neighborhoods have been built in a traditional gridiron pattern—that is, streets at right angles—newer neighborhoods wind, curve and dead-end their roadways to help slow speeds and minimize the through traffic. If you want more safety for your children and quieter living, look for cul-de-sacs, streets to nowhere and looping streets off main roads.

If your children ride bicycles, you will rest easier in an area with bike trails, pathways or at least sidewalks where they can get away from car traffic.

After checking out all these points carefully, you will be ready to start thinking about specific homes with the assurance that you are buying in a neighborhood where you will be happy. Right from the beginning you have made house hunting easier.

How the Agent Can Help

Your agent has most likely spent years studying the different neighborhoods in the area you are considering. Good agents know which areas are strong and which neighborhoods are getting hot. They know the areas that have gone up in value in a year and which areas may be coming down. Take advantage of this knowledge. After you have narrowed your choice to several neighborhoods, let your agent be your guide and chauffeur, so that you can sit back, take out your notebook, ask questions and learn.

☞ **Money-$aving Tip #9** *An experienced real estate agent who knows the area intimately can help you find a neighborhood that is likely to retain its character and value.*

Inspection Checklist

The following checklist will help you research and evaluate a potential neighborhood to be sure it's right for you and your family. Each "No" answer on the checklist may indicate a current or potential problem. The rating form following the checklist allows you to summarize your findings and to evaluate all the basic components of the neighborhood.

The Neighborhood

Yes   No

___ ___ 1. Is the neighborhood stable, as opposed to in decline?

___ ___ 2. Are homes well cared for?

___ ___ 3. Are the lawns well kept?

___ ___ 4. Are most homes in the area in the same price range?

___ ___ 5. Who lives there—are their ages, incomes, number of children, interests the same as yours?

___ ___ 6. Is the neighborhood quiet (i.e., no irritating noise levels from automobiles, trucks, air-planes, trains, buses, etc.)?

___ ___ 7. Is the neighborhood convenient to your employment?

___ ___ 8. Is public transportation available?

___ ___ 9. Is the neighborhood close to shopping, schools, churches, parks and recreation centers?

___ ___ 10. Is the neighborhood in a low crime area?

___ ___   11. Are property values rising?

___ ___   12. Have property taxes been steady in the past year or two?

___ ___   13. Are taxes in line with those in other areas?

___ ___   14. Is there adequate police and fire protection?

___ ___   15. Is there convenient emergency medical service?

___ ___   16. Does the area have plans for expansion and development?

___ ___   17. Does the area have any zoning restrictions?

___ ___   18. Have you checked whether any special assessments are anticipated?

___ ___   19. Are the schools of good quality?

___ ___   20. Are traffic patterns safe?

___ ___   21. Is there adequate street lighting?

___ ___   22. Do the surrounding houses conform architecturally?

Overall Rating   Good Fair Poor

	Good	Fair	Poor
Neighborhood	___	___	___
House location within neighborhood	___	___	___

Major Problems:

Commonly Asked Questions

Q. What kind of property will increase most in value?

A. The key factor is location. A house in a desirable location—one where people want to live and work—is always in demand, and it is in limited supply. In general, property values tend to increase at a pace at least equal to the inflation rate, but most homes—especially well-located, single-family homes—appreciate at a much higher rate.

Q. What things are important to consider when choosing a community in which to live?

A. Convenient shopping, banking and transportation, quality of fire and police protection, schools, garbage pickup, sewage system and other governmental services, quality and access to medical and recreational facilities, access to parks, houses of worship and workplaces, extent or absence of crime, zoning ordinances, extent of occupant ownership, property value levels, and general stability of the area—these are some of the considerations that are important to many people when they choose a community in which to live.

Q. How can you recognize what neighborhoods appeal to you, what areas are appreciating and what community you'd like to buy in?

You can learn to recognize a potentially good area by doing the following:

- Obtain background data on areas you are interested in from the Chamber of Commerce, the local banks and real estate offices.
- Drive and walk around the area to see negative as well as positive characteristics.

- Find an experienced real estate agent who knows the area and will share all this information with you.

Q. How can I find out what homes are selling for in a given neighborhood?

A. Home sales are a matter of public record. You can get all the information you need about recent sales, including prices and listing times, from the county Recorder of Deeds. Or ask your real estate agent to provide you with sales prices of houses in the area that are comparable to the home you are considering.

Q. What can be done about nearby environmental hazards?

A. The best protection against nearby hazards is to be aware of their presence *before* buying the house and to be alert to proposed changes in zoning that might allow hazards to develop once you own the property.

CHAPTER 3

Selecting the Site

After you've gotten a feel for the neighborhood, you'll need to really focus in on the lot. Begin with a survey of the grounds and the house from a distance to get an overall impression of the landscaping, driveway, walks, patios, decks, fences and other structures on the property. Does the site have any drawbacks that detract from the house? Is there a pleasing view? Does it have good drainage?

If you are serious about a house, take the time to visit the site several times during the day. Not all sites are as peaceful as they look. Evaluating the noise environment may save you lots of headaches later. Sometimes an area that is quiet at midday can become noisy in the evening or early in the morning. A site near a school playground is likely to be noisy several times during the day. Check out the activities of the neighbors. Car buffs and do-it-yourselfers may work on their noisy hobbies well into the night. And ask if major construction projects are planned for the neighborhood.

The sounds of heavy equipment are enough to rattle the dishes right off the shelf.

The site should be an integral part of the design of a house. Correct siting on the property can make the house more pleasant to live in and more attractive to buyers when it is placed on the market. The site should be analyzed for its topography (surface features of land), the variations in the sun's path from season to season, the types and sizes of trees, the views, the noise and the proximity to neighbors.

☞ **Money-$aving Tip #10** *Trees enhance the beauty and value of a lot and house.*

House Orientation

Orientation refers to the position and direction of the house on the site. A house that is properly oriented in relation to the sun has nature working for it all year round. It has been scientifically established that the south side of a house receives five times as much solar heat in the winter as in summer, and the north side receives no solar heat at all during winter months. So ideally, a house should be positioned on the lot so that the main living areas and the largest glass areas (windows and sliding glass doors) face *south.* By locating public living spaces, such as the living room, the family room, the dining room and the kitchen along the south side of the house, you can make use of the sun's light and energy during the day. Since the north side of the house receives no direct sunlight it may be a good location for private and unoccupied spaces, such as bedrooms, utility rooms and storage rooms.

Figure 3.1 shows how a roof overhang can shade summertime sun and also allow for winter-sun penetration. Because the summer sun rides high in the sky, a wide roof overhang will shade the windows by deflecting the direct

FIGURE 3.1 The Sun's Arc

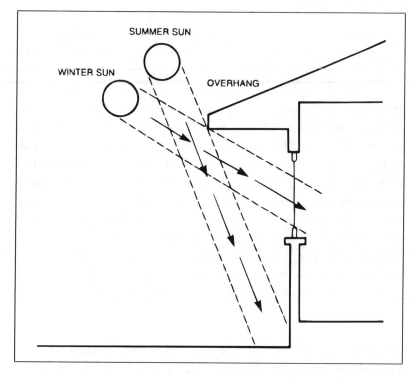

heat rays. A roof overhang will not interfere with the sunshine in winter months because the winter sun travels a much lower arc and shines in at a much lower angle than the summer sun.

View

A decision on the location of a house can also depend on the view. If the site has a scenic view to the east or west, such as a mountain, lake or golf course, it might be wise to take advantage of it, in spite of the sun factor.

Outdoor Space

With good site planning, outdoor space is designed for three different functions: *public use, service use* and *private use.* The *public zone* is the area visible from the street—usually the land in front of the house. Zoning regulations specify how far back a house must be placed on a lot. The *service zone* consists of the driveway, the walks and the areas where trash and garbage can be collected and outdoor equipment can be stored. It should be designed so that deliveries can be made to the service entrance without intrusion into space intended only for private use. The *private zone* is the outdoor living space for the family. It may include a patio, a garden, a deck, a barbecue pit and a play area for children. Creating an outdoor retreat is one of the most economical ways to add living space. Today's best new house designs anticipate this lifestyle and incorporate the outdoors with their interior spaces.

In most cases, a minimum amount of land should be allocated for public and service use and the maximum amount for private enjoyment. Thus, architects prefer to situate a house near the street to provide a larger backyard.

Drainage

You'll want to be careful about buying a house set in a hollow, depression or low-lying area. Although a home nestled in a little valley may be picturesque and enchanting, it would not be quite so charming if every heavy rain floods the place. Ideally, the drainage should be away from the home's foundation. That means the house should be situated on an elevated part of the lot. The best spot is a knoll from which land slopes away in all directions, as in Figure 3.2a. A gentle slope toward the street or road is also a good site arrangement. Drainage problems will occur when water

FIGURE 3.2 Land Slopes and Drainage

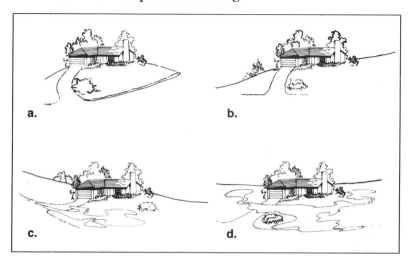

runs off across the site or down a slope toward the house, as in Figure 3.2b and c. Equally bad, and perhaps worse, is the site in Figure 3.2d, where water doesn't run off at all. Snow and ice can trap roof drainage around the perimeter of the house.

How *the Agent Can Help*

The most helpful source of factual information about areas, sites and homes is your real estate agent. Ask for your agent's opinion about such things as soil composition, the site's topography, easements, zoning or deed restrictions, building code requirements and the placement of the house on the lot. If not already known through personal knowledge, your agent can call on builders, surveyors, appraisers, engineers, inspectors and other specialists to answer any questions you might have.

☞ **Money-$aving Tip #11** *A house that's sited to take advantage of the sun, the wind and the topography costs less to heat and cool and can save thousands of dollars over the years in utility bills.*

Inspection Checklist

Lot Information
Orientation of House: N   S   E   W
Distance to Lot Boundaries: Front ____ Sides ____ Back ____
Other Structures: _____
Best/Worst Views: _____

Site and House Location

Yes   No

____ ____   1. Does the site have all the necessary utilities?

____ ____   2. Does the topography of the lot allow for good drainage?

____ ____   3. Is the property well landscaped?

____ ____   4. Does the landscaping afford privacy?

____ ____   5. Is the property free of easements or deed restrictions?

____ ____   6. Are you satisfied with the location of the site in terms of position in the block?

____ ____   7. Is the size of the lot satisfactory?

____ ____   8. Does the house take good advantage of natural conditions (sun, breeze, view)?

____ ____   9. Are the public, service and private zones of the lot well defined?

The Grounds

____ ____   10. Is the landscaping compatible with the architectural style of the house?

____ ____   11. Is the overall landscaping plan visually appealing?

____ ____   12. Have the grounds been well maintained?

____ ____   13. Does the land slope so that water drains away from the house and outdoor living areas?

____ ____   14. Are trees and shrubs far enough away from the house? (If they are too close, overhanging branches can cause serious damage to roofs, gutters and siding.)

____ ____   15. Are trees far enough away from the house so that roots cannot penetrate cracks in the foundation or lift up the paving on driveways and walks?

____ ____   16. Are trees healthy and at a safe distance from the house?

____ ____   17. Will landscaping maintenance require minimal work?

____ ____   18. If not, will extensive maintenance requirements be convenient for you?

____ ____   19. Has proper landscaping been done to prevent soil erosion?

____ ____   20. Does the driveway slope away from the house and garage?

____ ____   21. Are the driveway, walks and patio in good shape (no severe cracks, etc.)?

____ ____   22. Is the driveway exit unobstructed?

____ ____   23. Does the driveway provide a turnaround?

____ ____   24. Are outdoor living areas screened from public view?

____ ____   25. Are fences in good shape (no signs of deterioration such as wood rot, insect damage, rust)?

____ ____   26. Are wooden portions of patios, decks or porches free of rot or insect damage?

____ ____   27. Are walks, driveways or patios free of cracks that could cause accidents?

____ ____   28. Has the swimming pool been maintained properly? (Check the tiles around the pool, the pool walls and the pool bottom.)

____ ____   29. Do repairs appear to be minor rather than major?

____ ____   30. Is the pool decking intact and safe?

____ ____   31. Is the pump and filtration system in good working order?

____ ____   32. Do the skimmers work properly?

____ ____   33. Is there fencing (or a cage) around the pool area?

____ ____   34. Is the water in the pools clear and light blue in color?

____ ____   35. Are all wood deck components free of decay and insect activity?

____ ____   36. Are there cracked, missing, broken or loose flooring or railings?

____ ____   37. Is the deck free of safety hazards?

Overall Rating

	Good	Fair	Poor
Site	—	—	—
House location	—	—	—
Size of lot: ____ sq. ft.	—	—	—
Landscaping	—	—	—
Slope of land	—	—	—
Walks	—	—	—
Patios	—	—	—
Decks	—	—	—
Porches	—	—	—
Fences	—	—	—
Swimming pool	—	—	—

Major Problems:

Commonly Asked Questions

Q. What is the most common hazard in a residential neighborhood?

A. Heavy traffic. So, the fact that a house is located on a heavily traveled street may affect its resale value.

Q. What is meant by setback?

A. The minimum distance away from the street or sidewalk that a house may be built.

Q. What is a water table?

A. At some point below the earth's surface, the soil is saturated with water. The water table is the depth below the surface that this ground water begins.

Q. What are the three areas of a site?

A. Public use area, service use area and private use area.

Q. Most lots are rectangular, with less street frontage than depth. What is the recommended ratio?

A. A 1:3 ratio is recommended. This shape gives the greatest area of lot space with a minimum of expensive street paving.

CHAPTER 4

Reading a House's Vital Statistics

Some people love the openness of contemporary homes with living areas rather than traditionally walled rooms. Some people feel more comfortable in cozy spaces. Some want bold architectural details; others want their home to be a "background" that doesn't intrude at all. Some styles of architecture may please you more than others. If you have a strong preference, recognize it and try to find the home that fits.

Architectural Styles

Among the many features of a house, its architectural style is one of the first things to catch the eye and make an impression. Although construction details are rigidly specified by building codes, house styles may vary greatly. No absolute standards exist, and real estate values rest on what potential buyers think is desirable, as well as on what they consider to be attractive.

Homes today don't always fall into neat style categories. The outward appearance of a house may stick to one style only or a combination of several different styles. Figure 4.1 shows some house styles that have been popular for many years.

The architectural style of a home provides long-range appeal to users. The factors that affect appeal are hard to identify and differ according to style trends and individual preferences and tastes.

☞ **Money-$aving Tip #12** *Buying a house whose style is uniquely individual will probably minimize rather than maximize its resale value because the house will appeal to a somewhat more limited number of potential buyers.*

House Types

As you begin to explore the type of house you want, you'll discover many options. *House type* refers to the number and arrangement of a home's living levels. Although variations exist, most house types fall somewhere within the basic categories described below and as illustrated in Figure 4.2.

Ranch

The *ranch* is a one-story, low-to-the-ground structure with wide overhangs and all the habitable rooms on one level. A raised ranch has a basement area partly above ground, but stairs from outside usually lead directly to the main-level living area.

FIGURE 4.1 Architectural Styles

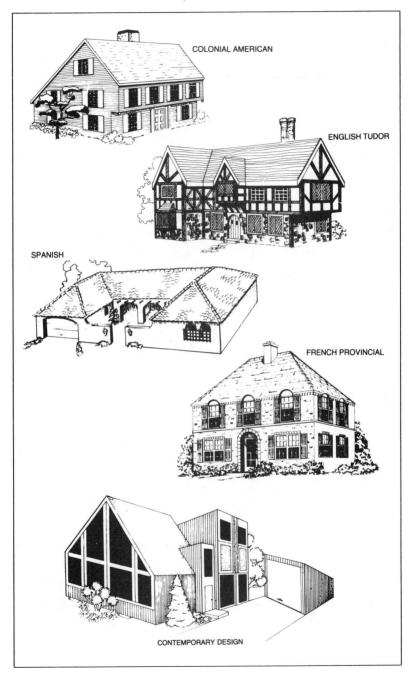

FIGURE 4.2 House Types

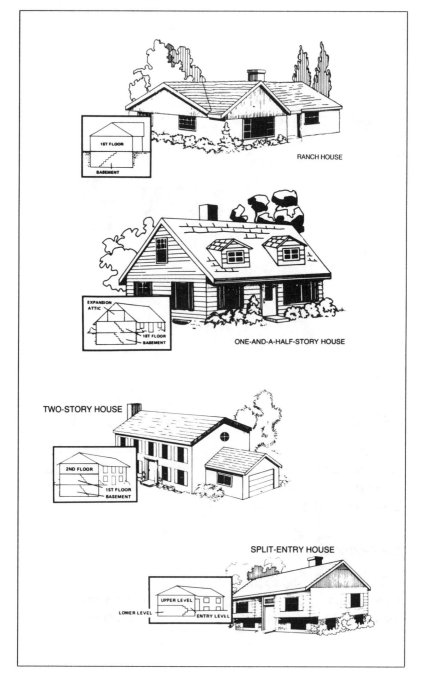

FIGURE 4.2 House Types (Continued)

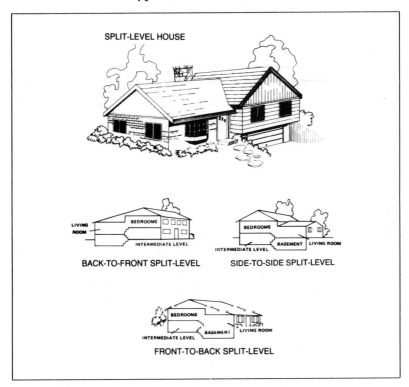

Split-Level

Generally, the *split-level* house has floors halfway between other floors. One floor is often partially below ground level. Variations include side-to-side split, back-to-front split and front-to-back split.

Split-Entry

This is a modified split-level. The entry is on grade or just a few steps above, with the main level half a flight up and the lower level half a flight down. Typically, the lower level is raised halfway out of the ground to admit natural light into the space and make the lower level more livable.

Story-and-a-Half

Often called a *Cape Cod,* this low-profile house has a full flight of stairs connecting two levels. The roofline usually starts at the first story and peaks to allow headroom in about half of the second-story space.

Two-Story

A house that has two complete stories, both out of the ground, connected by a full flight of stairs is a *two-story.* Entry is usually up a few steps from ground level. The two-story house offers the most living space within an established perimeter; the living area is doubled on the same foundation.

☞ **Money-$aving Tip #13** *Don't underestimate the inconvenience of a two-story house that doesn't have a bathroom downstairs. It's likely you will end up adding at least a half-bath before you move again.*

House Size

How much space do you need? Consider every detail of the house in terms of your lifestyle and your family's needs for space, privacy and appropriate layout. Are there enough bedrooms and baths? Homebuyers today consider three bedrooms and two bathrooms the minimum requirement in an average house. And the most important bedroom to buyers is the master suite, which is expected to be larger and more elaborate than other bedrooms in the house.

Do the kitchen layout and size meet your expectations? A majority of homebuyers say that a large kitchen is at the top of their priority list. The preferred layout is an L-shaped floor plan with either an island work area or a large space for a table and chairs. This would be in addition to a larger dining area.

Homebuyers assume that every house will have a living room. Family rooms also rank high in buyer preference.

Pay careful attention to the size of the rooms, and don't rely on your memory of how large they are. Even if the seller has given you a list of room sizes, they are not always accurate. Get out your tape measure and verify them.

Does the house have expansion possibilities? An unfinished basement or attic could become that additional room you need. A large lot may give you room to expand to the side or to the rear.

☞ **Money $aving Tip #14** *If you think you may need more space in the near future, be sure the house and lot allow for expansion.*

Older House versus Newer House

Older homes have a lot going for them. Often the neighborhood surrounding an older home is established and property values are stable. If you favor unique, individual architecture, an older home might satisfy your sense of beauty. Older homes can be absolutely charming with style refinements not available today. Older homes often offer more space for the money than newer homes. Ceiling heights, floor space and room sizes are generally on a grander scale than in newer homes.

The chronological age of a home may not be important if it has been well maintained throughout the years. As a matter of fact, with advancing age, homes seem to acquire a nebulous thing called "character."

But it's a fact that even well kept homes, as they get older, usually begin to have problems with wiring, heating and plumbing. And renovations and replacements can often prove more expensive and time consuming than they're worth. All things being equal, newer homes need less attention right away than do older homes. Whether to look for newer homes or older homes is something you have to decide. It all boils down to personal preference. New or old, your home should be a very personal reflection of your interests, your preferences and your lifestyle. Every home represents a bit of a compromise, even a custom-built home. You'll have to bend your way of living a little to the house; the house will have to give a little to your family.

☞ **Money-$aving Tip #15** *In an older house, be on the lookout for such problems as lead paint, asbestos, inadequate insulation, leaky pipes and an obsolete electrical system. The solutions can be expensive.*

Most Important Features List

Today's housing market offers a wide variety of homes in an equally wide variety of price ranges and locations. So most house hunters go with a prepared list of requirements, such as price range, number of bedrooms and number of baths. Once these features have been decided on, the search for the perfect house begins.

Before you contact a real estate agent, spend some time thinking about exactly what you want in a new home. Here is a checklist of things you should consider. Space is provided at the end of the list so you can enter additional features of interest to you.

Most Important Features Checklist

____ Price range

____ Square feet

____ Number of bedrooms

____ Number of bathrooms

____ Master suite

____ Fireplace

____ Central air-conditioning

____ A room that can be turned into an office

____ Living room

____ Family room

____ Formal dining room

____ Dining L

Kitchen layout:

____ Single-counter

____ L-shaped

____ U-shaped

____ Island

____ Laundry room

Garage:

____ One-car

____ Two-car

____ Carport

____ Storage room

_____ Den

_____ Wood deck

_____ Patio

_____ Swimming pool

_____ View

_____ _____

_____ _____

_____ _____

_____ _____

How the Agent Can Help

When you sit down with your real estate agent, outline your basic needs first, then discuss the things you'd like to have if you can afford them. Be sure to go over your preferences for styles of architecture and types of homes. There's no sense in looking at colonial homes if you have your heart set on a contemporary one. Being as open and candid as you can will help your agent match the right home to your needs.

Inspection Checklist

House style: traditional/contemporary
House type: one-story/one-and-a-half story/
                  two-story/split-level/split-entry/other
Age of house: _____

Yes   No

___   ___   1. Is the house style and type suitable for your lifestyle?

___   ___   2. Has the house been built by a reliable contractor?

___   ___   3. Is it covered by a warranty?

___   ___   4. Is the style consistent throughout, and the lines and detail in pleasing balance?

___   ___   5. Are materials, scale and proportion consistent with the architectural style?

___   ___   6. Does the house blend with surrounding homes?

___   ___   7. Does the house have expansion potential?

___   ___   8. Are the other houses in the neighborhood expensive enough so that the cost of improvements to your house can be recovered?

___   ___   9. Does the house have good resale potential? (Ask the real estate agent for up-to-date information on what's happening in the neighborhood.)

Overall Rating   Good   Fair   Poor

House type and style meet
  your needs   ___   ___   ___
Expansion potential   ___   ___   ___
Resale value   ___   ___   ___
Major Problems:

Commonly Asked Questions

Q. Should I buy a ranch or a multi-level house?

A. Which do you prefer? It's your choice. The great advantage of the one-story house is the absence of steps to climb or descend, except, perhaps, to a basement. And a one-story house is best adapted to indoor-outdoor living—porches, patios, terraces or swimming pools can be adjacent to any room. On the other hand, a multi-level house allows for more privacy with bedrooms on a different level than the rest of the living space.

Q. Which is cheaper to heat and cool—a two-story house or a one-story ranch with the same living space?

A. A two-story house. A house with a high ratio of interior space to exterior surface costs less to heat and to cool.

CHAPTER 5

Interior Design Strategies

The interior design or layout of a house is basic not only to day-to-day comfort and livability, but it affects the home's market value as well.

The Floor Plan

Two basic approaches to space are typically taken into account when designing a floor plan—open and casual, or separate and formal. In an open plan, fewer walls and use of half-height walls promote a sense of spaciousness. Activities can overlap from room to room. On the negative side, energy costs are usually increased, and often some privacy is lost. Fewer interior walls also can mean limited spots for furniture placement.

In a less-open plan, areas can be closed off to control sound or to direct heating and cooling. If more private areas are desired, natural light should be included on as many sides as possible to avoid a closed-in look. Spaces should flow well and not appear chopped up.

A good part of what makes a home seem comfortable is the arrangement of its rooms—they should be tailored to how you and your family will live in the space. Living with a floor plan that doesn't feel right or doesn't conform to a family's lifestyle is like wearing a shoe that doesn't fit. The family will never get used to it, and they will always wish they had something else. So before you decide on a floor plan, take a good look at the layout and imagine how it will feel living in the spaces. Observe how the layout moves (or hinders) traffic flow through the house. Will traffic lanes or windows and doors interfere with your likely furniture arrangement? Does the kitchen layout look workable? Is there adequate storage space? Will window locations capitalize on views and maintain privacy? Carefully analyzing a home's floor plan can help you get a realistic feel for what it would be like to live there every day.

A good floor plan directs traffic smoothly and usually divides neatly into three basic areas or zones: *working* or high-activity areas, *living* or moderate-activity areas, and *sleeping* or low-activity areas (see Figure 5.1). The *working zone* includes the kitchen, laundry area and perhaps a workshop and an office. The *living zone* consists of the living, dining and family rooms. The *sleeping zone* contains the bedrooms. Each zone should be separated from the others so that activities in one area do not interfere with those in another. Ideally, the areas that generate the most noise should be grouped together, well away from the bedrooms.

Circulation areas, consisting of halls, stairways and entries, often provide the key to a good floor plan. The main entry to the house should not open into any specific room but into a foyer or hall. Also, think of the view encountered from the entry. Entries, remember, are where a good many

FIGURE 5.1 Floor Plan with Zones and Circulation Areas

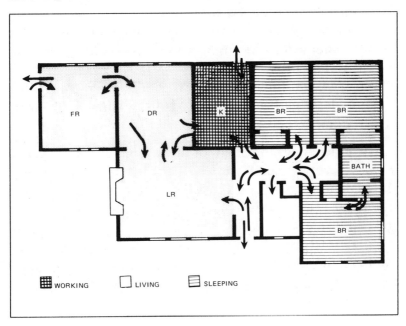

first impressions take shape, and the goal is to make a good first impression.

Another important consideration in any plan is quick access from the garage to the kitchen. Is there a short and convenient route for hauling groceries from the car into the house or taking out trash?

Key to the effectiveness of any floor plan is the efficient and convenient channeling of room-to-room traffic. Can people get directly from one room to another without crossing through other rooms? Is there direct access to a bathroom from any room? Is the stairway located off a hallway or foyer rather than off a room?

According to home shoppers, the design and location of the kitchen is a crucial part of their buying decision. A kitchen contains three main activity centers, as follows:

1. *Food storage*—includes the refrigerator/freezer, cabinets and counterspace
2. *Cooking*—includes the range, oven, counterspace on either side, and cabinets and drawers for pots, pans and utensils
3. *Cleanup*—includes the sink, counterspace on either side, a garbage disposal, a dishwasher and a trash compactor

The efficient arrangement of these three centers is called a *work triangle* (see Figure 5.2). For maximum efficiency, the triangle should have a total perimeter of at least 12 feet but no more than 22 feet. The room must be well ventilated to keep it free of cooking odors.

To save steps and time, short, direct routes should connect the kitchen with all eating areas. If traffic goes through the kitchen, it should pass outside the work triangle so people won't bump into each other when someone is carrying food.

For cooks who like to keep in touch with the family while preparing meals, a kitchen that's open to the family room should be considered. This arrangement makes the space seem larger and provides a place for quick countertop meals.

If a family enjoys entertaining, or appreciates dining variety, the floor plan must cater to an assortment of dining options, such as an informal eating area, breakfast bar or formal dining room. All these areas must be contiguous to a food-preparation and serving location. If the family likes to barbecue in the backyard, a plan with an outdoor deck or patio adjacent to the kitchen is ideal.

☞ **Money-$aving Tip #16** *Redoing a kitchen is likely to be expensive. So be sure of what you need and want before you buy.*

FIGURE 5.2 Kitchen Work Triangle

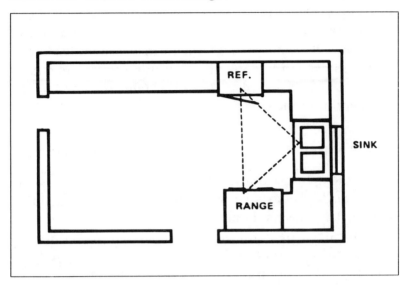

Whatever layout is chosen for the dining and living areas, plenty of space should be available for furnishings and activities. If entertaining in small groups is desired, a cozy family room would be more desirable than a formal living room. An intimate conversation or reading area is usually more possible, however, in a formal living room.

Privacy is the key to any successful bedroom arrangement. Sleeping areas should be secluded from living and working areas, especially for families with children or for those who entertain frequently.

In the master bath, locating the vanity in a separate area from the toilet, tub and shower makes it easier for a couple to get ready for the day. If a person enjoys relaxing after a stressful day by taking a hot bath, lifting weights or doing aerobics, the possibility of including a convenient exercise area, sauna or whirlpool tub should be considered.

A full bath near the secondary bedrooms adds to the convenience and privacy of other family members and overnight guests. A half-bath near the kitchen and living areas will keep guests from invading the home's private spaces.

Laundry facilities should be placed close to bedrooms and bathrooms. Proximity to the kitchen makes it convenient to wash and dry while cooking or cleaning there. As a compromise, it may be placed off the family room, in the basement or in the garage.

Master Suite

The most important bedroom to homebuyers is the *master suite.* Today's master suite often includes a sitting area, walk-in closets, home entertainment center and even a private deck or patio. And the *master bath* is bigger, better, more beautiful, and—whenever possible—more luxurious than ever before. Except for the kitchen, no other single room in the house reveals more about us—our culture, our socioeconomic system, our passion for gadgets—than does the bathroom.

Just think how dramatically the typical bath has changed in the past 15 or 20 years. From a closet-sized space with the basic tub, toilet and sink, the master bath has become a living area with plumbing. Bathrooms equipped with whirlpool tubs, combination shower/steam rooms and even bidets are becoming more common.

The bath of today is the rec room of the 1960s. More than a few have telephones, televisions, stereo systems, saunas, exercise equipment and tanning tables.

Storage Space

Storage space is an important consideration. A good floor plan will include a closet for every person in the family, a linen closet, a guest closet near the front door and, in colder climates, a closet near the rear door. Larger areas for building or repairing things, storing tools, bicycles and outdoor equipment, as well as bulk storage for "junk" are invaluable. The kitchen should have lots of storage space, all of it within convenient reach.

Basement

A basement provides low-cost space for heating and cooling equipment, bulk storage and so forth. Because the builder has to go below frost line with the foundation anyway, a basement adds little to the building cost in cold climates (but more as you go south).

If the building site slopes so that a ground-level entrance can be provided, a basement is good for workshops and family rooms. It stays cool in summer and warm in winter.

Garage

The location of the garage will affect the living patterns within the home. A garage can have any orientation, but the best place for it is on the west or north, where it can protect living space from the hot afternoon sun in summer and from howling winds in winter. More important than orientation, though, is convenience. A garage should be close to the kitchen; it should not block light out of other rooms. The garage should always be big enough for two cars. Even with small cars, it should have inside dimensions of at least 23 feet by 23 feet. Many home shoppers feel the garage should provide additional room for storage, a workbench or other activities.

Finding the Plan for You

Now you know the elements of good interior design. But you need more. In your search for that just-right floor plan, you need to review your activities and habits, your wish list and your dreams. Sit down with paper and pen and jot down absolutely every architectural element that turns you on. In other words, get your ideas down on paper. Next, make yourself a priority checklist that indicates the things you *must have* and the things you'd *like to have*. Remember, to find what you want in a house, it helps to know what you're looking for.

☞ **Money-$aving Tip #17** *A sound floor plan is a home's #1 selling point and adds to its resale value.*

How *the Agent Can Help*

Because agents work with houses every day, they probably know more about good and bad features of floor plans than any other source. If you have questions about the layout of the house you are inspecting, talk to your agent. A practical, efficient and flexible floor plan is important not only to your daily comfort, but also to the future marketability of the property.

Inspection Checklist

Room Sizes:
Living room   _____
Dining room   _____
Kitchen   _____
Family room   _____
Bedrooms   1 ____ 2 ____ 3 ____ 4 ____ 5 ____
Full bathrooms   1 ____ 2 ____ 3 ____
Half-baths   1 ____ 2 ____
Basement   _____
Garage   _____

Floor Plan

Yes   No

___ ___   1. Are main interior zones—living, working and sleeping—clearly separated?

___ ___   2. Does the front door enter into a foyer—not directly into a living area?

___ ___   3. Is there a front hall closet?

___ ___   4. Is there direct access from front door to kitchen, bathrooms and bedrooms without passing through other rooms?

___ ___   5. Is the rear door convenient to the kitchen and easy to reach from street, driveway and garage?

___ ___   6. Is a comfortable eating space for the family in or near the kitchen?

___ ___   7. Is a separate dining area or dining room convenient to the kitchen?

___ ___   8. Is a stairway located off of a hallway or foyer instead of off a room?

___ ___   9. Are bedrooms concealed from the living areas or foyer?

___ ___   10. Are walls between bedrooms soundproof? (They should be separated by a bathroom or closet.)

___ ___   11. Is the recreation room or family room well located?

___ ___   12. Is the basement accessible from the outside?

____ ____ 13. Are outdoor living areas accessible from the kitchen?

____ ____ 14. Are walls uninterrupted by doors and windows that could complicate furniture arrangement?

Kitchen

____ ____ 15. Is base cabinet storage space sufficient?

____ ____ 16. Is wall cabinet storage sufficient?

____ ____ 17. Is counterspace sufficient?

____ ____ 18. Is lighting sufficient?

____ ____ 19. Is there counterspace next to the refrigerator?

____ ____ 20. Is there enough window area?

____ ____ 21. Is the kitchen free of poorly placed doors that waste wall space?

____ ____ 22. Are work areas separate from heavy traffic areas?

____ ____ 23. Is there enough counterspace on either side of the sink?

____ ____ 24. Is there counterspace next to the range?

____ ____ 25. Are the sink, range and refrigerator arranged in a triangle?

____ ____ 26. Are they close enough together?

____ ____ 27. Is the kitchen modern enough?

____ ____ 28. Are there lights over work centers?

____ ____ 29. Are appliances in working order and relatively new (7 years or less)?

Miscellaneous Things To Look For

____ ____ 30. Does the exhaust system vent to the outside?

____ ____ 31. Does the exhaust fan operate properly?

____ ____ 32. Does the house have at least one full bathroom on each floor?

____ ____ 33. Is there at least one bathroom for every two people?

____ ____ 34. Is there adequate closet space throughout the house?

____ ____ 35. Is the laundry area in a satisfactory location?

____ ____ 36. Does the garage have direct access to the kitchen?

____ ____ 37. How many smoke detectors are there?

____ ____ 38. Are they working properly?

____ ____ 39. Are they properly located?

Exterior

____ ____ 40. Check the roof shingles. Are they in good shape (no broken, missing or deteriorating sections)?

____ ____ 41. Is the roof free of any signs of leaks?

____ ____ 42. Are the gutters and downspouts in good condition?

____ ____ 43. Do the downspouts carry water away from the house?

____ ____ 44. Are exterior walls straight (no bulging)?

____ ____ 45. Is the foundation free of signs of defects?

___ ___ 46. Are all sections of siding firm?

___ ___ 47. Is the siding in good shape (no missing or decaying sections)?

Garage

___ ___ 48. Are the garage siding and trim in good condition (no peeling paint or faded colors)?

___ ___ 49. Is the garage floor free of any major cracks?

___ ___ 50. Is the garage floor sealed to prevent water penetration and stains?

___ ___ 51. Are all walls free of watermarks or other signs of water penetration?

___ ___ 52. Do the doors open and close properly?

___ ___ 53. Can the doors be locked?

___ ___ 54. Is there an automatic door opener? (If so, check to see if it works.)

___ ___ 55. In an attached garage, inspect the door from the garage to the house. Is it fireproof?

___ ___ 56. Are the interior walls and ceiling adjacent to living spaces fireproof?

___ ___ 57. In an attached garage, is the floor of the garage lower than the house slab? (This prevents toxic gases from entering the house.)

___ ___ 58. Is there a piece of protective weatherstripping between the base of the door and the ground?

___ ___ 59. Is the garage wide and long enough?

Overall Rating

	Good	Fair	Poor
Floor plan	——	——	——
Room sizes	——	——	——
Kitchen	——	——	——
Bathrooms	——	——	——
Living room	——	——	——
Dining room	——	——	——
Family room			
Bedrooms	——	——	——
Master suite	——	——	——
Closets	——	——	——
Storage	——	——	——
Laundry area			
Basement	——	——	——
Garage	——	——	——

Major Problems:

Commonly Asked Questions

Q. What do home shoppers consider to be the single-most desirable feature in a house?

A. Fireplaces rank highest in buyer preference, followed by large kitchens and then family rooms.

Q. What is the best way to know if a house plan will fit your lifestyle?

A. Mentally track your daily activities through the house or plan you are considering. Start by making sure the essentials are there. Soon you'll be able to determine when a floor plan is right for your way of life.

Q. How many bedrooms should I be considering?

A. Home shoppers consider three bedrooms the minimum requirement in an average house. Fewer than 10 percent of prospective buyers indicate that they would even be interested in looking at a two-bedroom house. This suggests that an extra bedroom or two will make your home more appealing to a larger number of interested buyers when it comes time to sell.

Q. Should the house open into a foyer?

A. Yes. Buyers prefer having a separate foyer or hall leading into the house so guests do not have to enter directly into a living area.

Q. What is the primary concern about where the dining room is located?

A. The dining room must be convenient to the kitchen.

CHAPTER 6

The Fundamentals of Foundations

In this chapter and others to follow, many construction terms and concepts will be presented and discussed. Whenever you feel the need, refer to the *House Diagram* in the Appendix.

Foundation

A *foundation* (see Figure 6.1) supports the weight of the house and its contents. Anchored below ground to hold the house steady, the foundation keeps the wood structure above grade to prevent decay and insect damage.

A bad foundation may cause excess shifting and settlement of the house. This can result in cracks in foundation walls, cracks in finished walls and ceilings, uneven floors, and doors and windows that don't fit properly.

FIGURE 6.1 Foundation

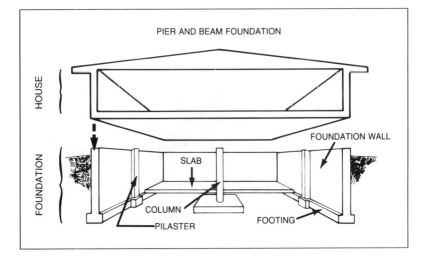

Footing

The foundation consists of two parts: the *footing* and the *walls*. The footing supports the foundation walls and is designed to distribute the home's weight over the ground. The footing is typically made of concrete and is placed below the frost line to hold the house in place as freezing and thawing temperatures cause the soil to heave.

Foundation Walls

Foundation walls form an enclosure for basements or crawl spaces. They also carry wall, floor, roof and other building loads. Most concrete walls are made of poured concrete or concrete block that rest on concrete footings (see Figures 6.2 and 6.3).

Poured Concrete. Poured concrete foundation walls are created within forms that are removed after the cement hardens. They are considered stronger and able to bear heavier loads than block foundations. They're also better

FIGURE 6.2 Poured Concrete Foundation Wall

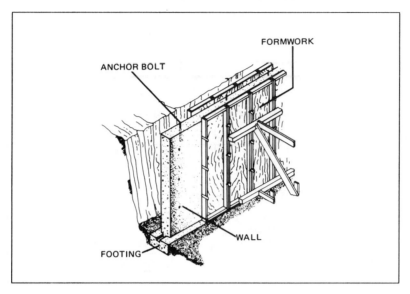

barriers against water seepage, air infiltration and insects. Underground moisture and expansive soils are good reasons for a poured concrete foundation.

For houses that have basements, the height between the basement floor to the bottom of the floor joists above is usually about 7 or 8 feet. In a crawl space, the height is about 3 feet to 4 feet.

Concrete Block. Concrete blocks are laid row by row to form a foundation wall. They're considered easier to work with and repair than poured concrete walls, but more prone to cracking, which allows air, moisture, water and insects inside. They can be filled with concrete and reinforced with steel bars to add strength.

Slab Foundations

Slabs are built on footings for support, although some slabs, known as "floating slabs," are built without footings.

FIGURE 6.3 Concrete Block Foundation Wall

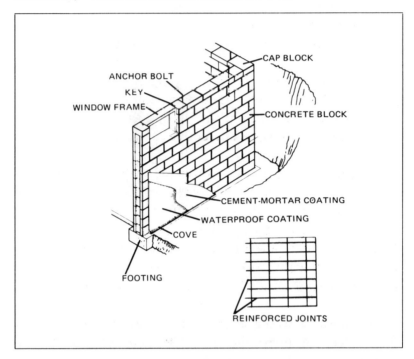

Slab foundations make sense where there is high ground water or bedrock close to the surface. They are usually simple and inexpensive to install, but they don't allow for a basement.

Recognizing Foundation Structural Defects

Walk around the perimeter of the house and inspect the foundation. The foundation should be exposed for 6 inches to 8 inches aboveground. Pay particular attention to any areas that appear to be settling. Settlement is caused by the compression of soil under the foundation. All houses settle. The uneven settlement of the foundation, especially at the corners, however, is a sure sign of trouble. Uneven settlement is evidenced also by cracks in foundation walls, cracks in finished walls and ceilings, floors that slope, and windows and doors that fit poorly.

Most hairline cracks in the foundation are surface cracks indicating minor stresses and are not serious. On the other hand, vertical cracks that are wider at the top than the bottom, called V-cracks, are something to worry about. V-cracks are signs that point to a settlement problem. And at some point, expensive corrective action usually must be taken.

Long horizontal cracks on outside walls can be serious. These kinds of cracks usually occur because the gutters and downspouts are spilling runoff water too close to the foundation. Repairing the gutters and downspouts and increasing the grad (the slope of the soil away from the house) will usually correct the problem. The force of tree roots can also produce large horizontal cracks and bulges.

☞ **Money-$aving Tip #18** *Don't buy a home with foundation problems. Although most foundation problems can be corrected, repair work is usually expensive.*

Check for signs of water penetration. Peeling paint on a concrete foundation may indicate moisture buildup in the basement. Soil should be graded away from the foundation to allow runoff water to flow away from the house. Look for signs of runoff pooling against the foundation. Check to see that downspouts have splash plates to channel water away.

Inspecting the Basement

A basement is the lowest level of a house and usually is left unfinished by the builder. The exterior walls of a basement also are the foundation walls of the house. Exposed foundation walls can tell you a lot about the structural soundness of the house. For example, curves or bows in the foundation walls may indicate excessive weight being applied to that area.

Does the basement smell musty or feel damp? Look for signs of water penetration—discoloration along the lower wall surfaces, damp wood sills (these rest on the foundation and support the wall framing) or discoloration of framing members.

Check the location of any foundation cracks identified on your external examination. Does water appear to have entered through them? A leaky basement is one of the biggest headaches a homeowner can have and often is difficult and expensive to correct.

☞ **Money-$aving Tip #19** *The first step and usually the most effective method of preventing basement water leakage is to control rain and roof runoff water that reaches within 10 feet of the foundation. This can be done by extending the gutter downspouts and by building up the grade against the foundation.*

Termites and Other Wood Destroyers

Before concrete for the foundation was poured, the ground should have been chemically treated to poison termites—ant-like insects that are very destructive to wood. This prevents them from coming up through or around the foundation and into the wooden structure. The chemical treatment of the lumber used for sills and beams and the installation of metal termite shields also provides protection.

When checking for termites, look for fuzzy sand- or earth-colored, tube-shaped columns snaking up the foundation. Termites and wood rot can destroy wood from inside, with little visible evidence. Examine any wood adjacent to the foundation, such as siding or porch supports. If you question its soundness, probe it with a screwdriver. If the wood feels like cork, it has been eaten away on the inside.

Carpenter ants and powder-post beetles are other insects that cause damage to wood. Damage by carpenter ants can be recognized by the presence of hollow, irregular, clean chambers cut across the grain of partially decayed wood. The most obvious sign of powder-post beetles are small round holes in the infested wood. The beetles exit through these holes after they have done their work.

Moisture in Homes

As a homeowner, you should be aware of the symptoms of moisture problems, how to identify the sources of moisture and how to deal with any problems. Not only will you protect your home from damage, but you also will provide a healthier environment for your family, because excess moisture promotes the growth of molds and bacteria.

Symptoms of Moisture Problems

Excess moisture is the primary cause of wood decay and wood-destroying insects. There are many symptoms of excess moisture in a home. *Condensation* on windows, walls or other smooth surfaces signals either excess moisture or the need to insulate or warm the surface in question. *Musty odors* may indicate mold, mildew or rot. Also, household odors that seem to linger may signal that ventilation in the house must be increased. *Rot* and *wood decay* indicate advanced moisture damage. But unlike surface mold and mildew, wood decay fungi penetrate, soften and weaken the wood. *Peeling, blistering* or *cracking paint* may indicate that moisture from outside or inside the home is damaging the wood or siding. If the raw wood can be seen between paint cracks or under blisters, the cause is most likely excess moisture. *Corrosion* and *rust* on metal are sure signs that moisture is at work. Finally, *concrete* and *masonry efflorescence,* a white powdery substance left after moisture has moved through a masonry foundation or basement wall, indicate that ground moisture is entering the basement.

Identifying the Sources of Moisture

Moisture arises from both inside and outside the home. Outdoor moisture sources usually result from poor drainage and blocked air circulation near the house, and high outdoor humidity. An important transfer of moisture from outside to inside the house takes place when windows are opened at night to allow fresh air to enter. Night air often has a high relative humidity. Indoor moisture is produced by plants and by people showering, washing, cleaning and cooking. In addition, plumbing leaks provide a steady source of moisture, particularly if the moisture stands or soaks into building materials.

Protection Against Excess Moisture

A high ground water table may cause problems by forcing moisture up through the ground into the basement or crawl space. This moisture then moves up through the house.

A well-built house uses waterproofing material, called a *vapor barrier,* to prevent this from happening. It is usually a thick polyethylene sheet laid on the earth underneath the house. In slab construction, the barrier is between the concrete floor and the layer of gravel spread over the ground. Although the barrier is completely hidden in slab or basement houses, it should be visible in crawl spaces. Clay drain tiles laid along the outer base of the foundation wall leading away from the house are another protection against basement water.

Combatting the sources of excess moisture may be as easy and inexpensive as fixing all leaking plumbing. However . . .

☞ **Money-$aving Tip #20** *Before you buy a house that may have a wet basement problem, get a good, unbiased diagnosis from a professional with moisture control experience. The solution could be costly.*

How the Agent Can Help

You may need to have tests conducted to check for termites or for the presence of radon gas. In fact, most financial institutions require a termite inspection before a conventional loan can be granted. Ask your agent for information about these tests and the businesses in the area that perform them.

Inspection Checklist

Yes   No

___   ___   1. Is the house situated on an elevated part of the lot for good drainage?

___   ___   2. Does water flow away from the house (not settle into the foundation)?

___   ___   3. Are the foundation walls free of vertical cracks?

—— ——   4. If cracks exist, are they hairline cracks? (Be sure they are not "V" cracks, as these could be part of a serious structural problem.)

—— ——   5. From the crawl space, is the foundation free of large cracks?

—— ——   6. Are piers in the crawl space firm and free of large cracks?

—— ——   7. Does the crawl space have adequate ventilation?

—— ——   8. Are foundation walls straight? (Make sure there are no obvious curves or bows.)

—— ——   9. Does the house (with a basement) have a foundation drain system; that is, gravel and pipe that lead water away from the house?

—— ——   10. Are there properly installed vapor barriers?

—— ——   11. Does the house smell clean (not musty)?

—— ——   12. Are the basement walls dry?

—— ——   13. Does the slab floor feel dry?

—— ——   14. Are the roof, windows and walls free of leakage warning signs?

—— ——   15. Has there been a recent termite check by an exterminator?

—— ——   16. Are wood beams and surfaces free of termites or wood rot?

—— ——   17. Are the floors firm? (Squeaks might be part of a serious structural problem.)

___ ___ 18. Are the floors level? (Make sure they don't sag or slope.)

___ ___ 19. Has the house been tested for radon gas?

___ ___ 20. Is the radon level within safe standards?

___ ___ 21. Are the ceilings level? (Make sure they don't sag.)

___ ___ 22. Does the house have a problem with excess moisture?

Overall Rating

	Good	Fair	Poor
Foundation	___	___	___
Drainage/site	___	___	___
Radon gas level	___	___	___
Termites and other insects	___	___	___
Wood rot	___	___	___
Excess moisture	___	___	___
Major Problems:			

Commonly Asked Questions

Q. What things should you look for in evaluating the foundation of a house?

A. Watch out for

- a diagonal crack that shows signs of recent movement,
- a large crack (one your finger can fit into),
- a vertical crack on any wall,
- a long horizontal crack on an outside wall or
- a slant or bulge on any wall.

Q. What can be done about excessive moisture in the home brought on by normal activities such as cooking and bathing?

A. Use the exhaust fans in the kitchen and bathrooms if you have them and consider installing them if you don't. Make sure the fans are powerful enough to remove moist air within a short period of time. Bathroom fans should run for at least 15 minutes after a shower or bath.

Q. What is the function of foundation walls?

A. Foundation walls must not only transfer the weight of the house to the footings but must also resist the forces against them from the earth outside.

Q. Can tree roots damage foundations?

A. Yes, but it usually takes a sizable root and very close proximity to bulge or crack a foundation wall. It is rare when a tree further than 5 feet away will exert enough pressure against a foundation to do damage. Roots can, however, absorb moisture from beneath footings during very dry weather and cause houses to settle.

Q. What is likely to happen if footings are too small?

A. Footings must be large enough and strong enough to support the loads imposed on them. Undersized or under-strength footings can allow house movements and even foundation failure.

Q. How destructive are carpenter ants?

A. Carpenter ants usually do only superficial damage to houses. The ants seem to prefer moist wood and make their homes in it. Fascia boards behind gutters, porch posts and deck beams are favorite spots.

C H A P T E R 7

Examining
Roofs, Chimneys
and Fireplaces

A roof can make a striking difference in the look and value of any home. And, along with the siding, it's the first line of defense against the elements—rain, snow, hail, sleet, sunshine, wind and temperature extremes.

Figure 7.1 shows some of the more common roof types or designs.

☞ **Money-$aving Tip #21** *A roof that complements the style of a home and is carefully maintained adds to the home's visual appeal and its resale value.*

Roof Coverings

There's a wide variety of roofing materials to choose from, including asphalt shingles, wood shingles and shakes, tile, metal and slate.

FIGURE 7.1 Roof Types

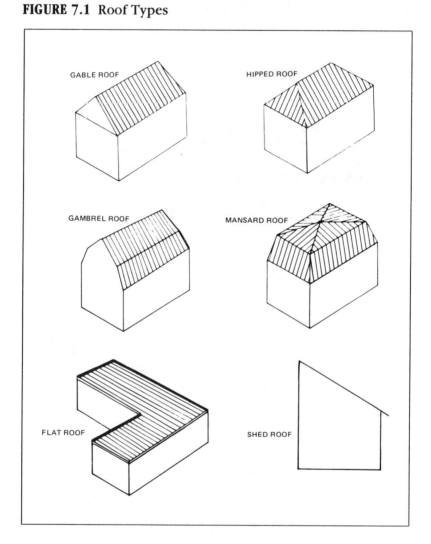

Asphalt Shingles

Asphalt shingles are asphalt-soaked felt coated with mineral granules. The most durable ones include fiberglass. Numerous colors are available—even wood imitations.

Asphalt is fire resistant and can last 15 to 30 years, depending on the quality.

Wood Shingles and Shakes

Wood shingles are smooth; shakes are hand-split and rough and have a much more rustic appearance. Cedar or redwood shingles can be natural, stained or painted and can last 20 to 50 years. Some areas of the country consider wood roofs a fire risk, even if treated.

Tile

Clay was the first material used for roof tiles, and, in this country, it is still the most popular. Clay tiles are durable, relatively expensive and heavy—requiring a stronger roof structure to support the additional weight. They will last indefinitely as long as the fasteners don't rust away.

Concrete tiles are lighter and less expensive than real clay tiles. Imitations of real clay tiles, slate, wood shakes and wood shingles are all available in concrete.

Metal

Metal is often aluminum, steel or copper. It comes as shingles, or as corrugated, ribbed or flat strips. Metal can be painted, coated in vinyl-plastic, or natural. It is resistant to fire, but can be damaged by wind-blown objects. Aluminum can last 35 years; copper even longer.

Slate

Slate is the ideal roofing material. It won't corrode or burn, and for the most part, it won't wear out. Given that slate is already a couple of million years old, it isn't asking a lot to expect it to last another hundred years or so on a house—as long as the fasteners that hold the slates to the roof don't fail. But a slate roof is expensive.

☞ **Money-$aving Tip #22** *A light-colored roof reflects heat and is best in areas where air-conditioning is the greater energy user. In colder climates, a dark roof is preferable because it absorbs more heat. In temperate climates, a middle-range shade is best.*

Inspecting the Roof

The sunny south can be like heaven, but it's rough on roofs. Asphalt shingles, for instance, begin to break down when the ceramic "pebbles" that protect their surfaces are dislodged or worn away. Direct sunlight then hardens the asphalt, which eventually cracks and splits, allowing water to slip through. Because of the difference in sun exposure, an asphalt shingle roof can be expected to last considerably longer, in, say, Illinois than in Florida. So be especially attentive about the condition of the roof on a house you're considering buying in a hot climate.

Using a ladder or binoculars, take a close look at the roof. Note any missing shingles or tiles and the general condition of the roof and the flashing at roof joints, valleys and vent pipes. *Flashing* refers to those materials, usually metal, that join different parts of the house to the roof. Valley refers to the angle formed by the meeting of two sloping sides of a roof.

Examine the gutters and downspouts for debris and leaks, as well as loose or broken support brackets. A good gutter and downspout system carries water away from the house. Without such a system, water will soak the ground near the foundation and is likely to run into the basement or crawl space of the house. In addition, a faulty gutter system will allow water and ice to back up under shingles along the eaves, which can cause leaks in the house and wood rot on the roof.

Water that gets into your house and stays there can gradually weaken and deteriorate the whole structure. This damage is much more difficult to repair than to prevent, so keep your eyes open for early signs of trouble.

Poke underneath the eaves (if wood) with a screwdriver to see if the wood is still firm. Soft wood is a sign of rot.

Check the attic ceiling for water stains, which indicate rain is seeping in through holes in the roof. Most leaks are difficult to pinpoint, though, because water usually runs down rafters far from where it entered. If you find water stains, it is prudent to have a roofing professional or home inspector locate these hidden leaks.

☞ **Money-$aving Tip #23** *A large percentage of homes on the market need a new roof or will need one within a year or two. And roofs are expensive to repair or replace.*

Inspect the attic ventilation system to make sure it's adequate. If the attic is not properly ventilated, problems with moisture are likely to develop. And dampness can breed dry rot, a fungus that deteriorates wood. Eave vents—openings under the eaves—combined with roof vents or gable vents are effective ways to create a positive movement of air out of the attic.

Also, moisture can collect and leak through ceilings below. In either case, you would need to talk to a ventilation expert about adding vents.

☞ **Money-$aving Tip #24** *Attic ventilation can greatly reduce home cooling costs, since temperatures in an unventilated attic can reach 145°F on a hot summer day. The temperatures in a ventilated attic will not exceed 115°F. A cooler attic results in cooler living areas.*

Chimneys

Every house with a fireplace or a heating system fueled by gas, oil, coal or wood needs a chimney (except those with high-efficiency furnaces). The main job of a chimney is to supply fresh air to the fire and to carry off smoke and harmful gases. An upward flow of air is caused by the temperature difference between the heated air in the chimney and the cold air outside.

Fireplaces

Before the first match is ever struck, a fireplace fills any room with warmth. Traditionally, fireplaces served as gathering places in the home. They still retain such focus today, as architectural points of interest and anchors for furniture grouping and room decor.

The desire for a fireplace has little or nothing to do with heating a home. Only about 10 percent of the heat produced from the burning wood makes it into the room—the rest is lost up the chimney. Rather, people want a fireplace for aesthetic appeal and the psychological impact created by a flickering, crackling fire.

Traditional wood-burning fireplaces fall into two general categories. Masonry fireplaces are hand built, brick-by-brick, from the ground floor up through the roof. These usually feature a clay liner and cost about four times as much as a prefabricated fireplace. Prefabricated models are metal, self-contained units lined with a synthetic material called refractory brick. They are commonly used in new construction and are safe and efficient in addition to being less expensive.

Exterior ornamentation for fireplaces is where choice really comes in. Brick, slate, tile, stone, wood and marble represent only a fraction of materials used. Architectural

FIGURE 7.2 Principal Parts of a Masonry Fireplace

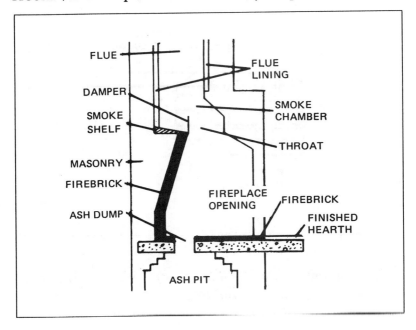

antiques are often incorporated, along with unusual mantels made of everything from polished brass to lucite.

A typical fireplace (see Figure 7.2) has a single opening with a damper and a hearth. The damper has a hinged lid that opens or closes to control the draft. The damper is located inside the fireplace at the top where it joins the chimney. Because fireplaces are difficult to construct, many are badly made and function poorly. One common problem is downdraft, where smoke is blown into the house by the wind outside. This can happen if the chimney does not extend at least 2 feet above any part of the roof within 10 feet of the chimney.

A buyer should request a fireplace inspection when purchasing a home that has a fireplace. Safety and working condition are best reported by a reputable fireplace company or licensed chimney sweep.

FIGURE 7.3 Chimney Cap

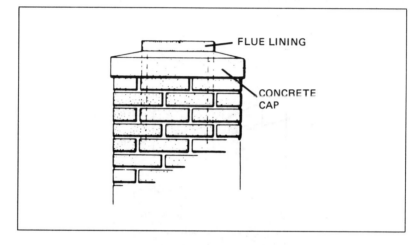

☞ **Money-$aving Tip #25** *Keep your fireplace damper closed unless you have a fire going. An open damper in a 48-inch square fireplace can let up to 8 percent of your heat out the chimney.*

Inspecting the Chimney and Fireplace

To inspect a chimney, begin by visually examining the exterior for cracks and damaged masonry. These can not only leak combustion gases indoors, creating a fire hazard, but they can also admit moisture into the brickwork from outdoors, speeding up deterioration.

Examine the condition of the chimney cap (Figure 7.3). It should be watertight to prevent moisture from entering between the brick and flue lining. Also inspect flashing around the base of the chimney (Figure 7.4). The installation of flashing around the chimney prevents water from entering the house.

FIGURE 7.4 Chimney Flashing

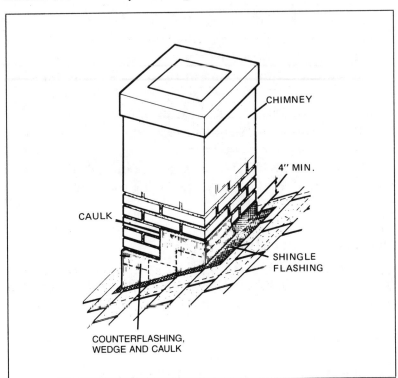

Check the condition of the bricks and mortar joints on the facing of the fireplace. Inside the fireplace, check for cracked or crumbling mortar joints between firebricks. Pay particular attention to the damper. Smoke in the chimney can back up into the room if the damper isn't operating properly, or if the chimney is clogged. You can tell how well the chimney draws by lighting a piece of paper in the fireplace and observing whether the smoke rises steadily and easily. Be sure the damper is fully open!

How the Agent Can Help

An agent's professional expertise can be of help throughout the inspection process. Let's create this scenario: You like a house and it checks out pretty well—except for the roof. In your opinion, it's on its last legs and will need to be replaced in a year or two.

Negotiation is one of the valuable skills an agent can offer you. An agent can perhaps work out a deal where the seller shares the cost of replacing the roof.

Inspection Checklist

Roof type: gable/hipped/gambrel/mansard/flat/other
Roof covering: asphalt shingles/wood shingles/wood shakes/tile/slate/metal/other
Gutters and downspouts: aluminum/galvanized metal/wood

Age of roof: _____

Roof and Gutters

Yes   No

___ ___   1. Look along the outer edges of the roof. Are the shingles firm (not curled or drooping)?

___ ___   2. Are all shingles, slates or tiles in good shape (none missing, cracked or broken)?

___ ___   3. Is the roof in good shape (no evidence of roof leaks)?

___ ___   4. Are flashings on the roof-mounted members in good condition?

___ ___   5. The greatest roof damage tends to occur in the valleys. Are the valleys undamaged and in good condition?

___ ___   6. Is the roof free of dark patches, which indicate weak spots?

___ ___   7. Are the wood shingles or shakes free of any signs of decay or rot?

___ ___   8. Check the overhang of the roof. Is it free of any signs of wood rot?

___ ___   9. Check inside the attic for leaks. Are all rafters free of water stains and any other signs of water penetration?

___ ___   10. Does the house have proper roof ventilation?

___ ___   11. Are roof vents free of any signs of water penetration?

___ ___   12. Are there gutters and downspouts on the house?

___ ___   13. Are the soffits, gutters and downspouts made of aluminum?

___ ___   14. If not, have they been recently painted?

___ ___   15. Did you see the house in the rain (the best time to check the roof and the gutter/downspout system)?

___ ___   16. Are all gutters free of leaks, cracks or weak spots?

___ ___   17. Are the gutters firm (not sagging)?

___ ___   18. Are the downspouts attached to the gutters, and do they carry water away from the house?

_____ _____ 19. Check the chimney. Are all bricks firmly in place? Is the chimney free of cracks?

_____ _____ 20. Is the chimney flashing in good condition?

Chimney and Fireplace

_____ _____ 21. Has the owner properly maintained and serviced the chimney and fireplace?

_____ _____ 22. Does the fireplace have a damper?

_____ _____ 23. Is the damper tight-fitting and easy to open and close?

_____ _____ 24. Does the fireplace draw well?

_____ _____ 25. Are the face bricks on the fireplace solid (not coming loose from the wall)?

_____ _____ 26. Are all firebricks firm?

_____ _____ 27. Is grout firm (not loose or crumbling)?

_____ _____ 28. Is the mantel on the fireplace level? (If not, be sure the reason is something other than a footing problem.)

Overall Rating	Good	Fair	Poor
Roof covering	___	___	___
Roof vents	___	___	___
Gutters and downspouts	___	___	___
Chimney	___	___	___
Fireplace	___	___	___
Major Problems:			

Commonly Asked Questions

Q. Are metal roofs noisy during rain storms?

A. Manufacturers say that any well-insulated roof with solid sheathing will control noise for people inside.

Q. Where do most roofing leaks occur?

A. The most common places where roof leaks occur are flashing around chimneys, flashing around plumbing pipes or attic fans that extend through the roof, and flashing in valleys where two roof surfaces come together.

Q. Can real clay tile be used on a house with standard framing?

A. If a house wasn't originally built to handle a clay roof, it would have to be reinforced to withstand the weight.

Q. What does "ice damming" mean?

A. When ice from intermittent thawing and refreezing of snow collects on the eaves of a roof, water from thawing ice and snow above it backs up under eaves and shingles. The melted snow and ice then saturate the wood framing, setting the stage for deterioration and decay.

Q. Can an asphalt shingle roof be overlaid with another asphalt shingle roof?

A. In almost all cases, an asphalt shingle roof can be installed over an old layer of shingles. Most codes require you to take up the roofing if two or more layers already cover the decking. There are two reasons for this: (1) the combined weight of the various layers may be too great for the decking, and (2) it may be difficult to fasten the new roofing securely through the previous layers. However, in colder climates and where roofs are strong and steep, it is not uncommon to find three and even four layers of asphalt shingles without any significant damage to the structure. But to be wind resistant, the roofing nails must penetrate well into the decking, which is now a good distance below the upper shingle surface. Quite often the nails don't reach into the wood.

CHAPTER 8

Checking Exterior Walls

The exterior appearance of the house is one of the first things a potential buyer will notice. It must look good and stand up to climatic conditions, too.

Real estate agents recognize the importance of the first impression and refer to it as *curb appeal.* A house with curb appeal puts the prospective buyer in the right mood to pay close attention to a sales pitch. The prospective buyer is attracted by the outside appearance of the house and grounds, and is hoping to find other virtues on the inside that will convince him that the first impression gave an accurate picture of the desirability of the place.

The exterior wall should be appropriate to the style of the house and should harmonize with its surroundings—the landscape and other homes in the neighborhood. The most popular exterior wall finishes fall into three general categories: siding, brick and stone veneer, and stucco.

Siding

Solid Wood

Solid lumber is the aristocrat of wood sidings. Cedar and redwood resist rot, so they can be left to weather. Other types of wood should be stained or painted. Solid wood siding can last the lifetime of the house.

Cedar Shingles and Shakes

Wood shingles have a smooth, uniform surface. Shakes are split and have a deeply textured face. Both are usually purchased unfinished, but can have factory-applied colors. Shingles fall into the moderate price range; shakes are more expensive. Both can last 50 years or more.

Aluminum

Aluminum siding comes in both vertical and horizontal styles, and in a wide range of colors and textures (including baked enamel). It's fireproof and impervious to insects, but noisy in wind, rain or hail if not insulated. The primary advantages of aluminum are its long life and its relatively low maintenance. However, it can be dented easily.

Vinyl

Vinyl siding comes in horizontal or vertical styles, with colorants that extend entirely through. Vinyl does not dent like aluminum, but it is brittle when subjected to extreme cold. Vinyl can last a lifetime and it is virtually maintenance free.

Plywood

Plywood is made of thin sheets of real wood bonded with waterproof adhesive. It may need periodic refinishing, but can last the lifetime of a house.

Hardboard

Hardboard is made by compressing wood fibers at high temperatures into sheet goods. Available in both horizontal and vertical styles, it features a uniform embossed surface (it's knot and grain free) and can be factory finished. Vinyl-clad hardboard carries guarantees up to 30 years.

Brick and Stone Veneer

Brick and stone veneers are expensive but can increase the market value of a home. They are popular because they are attractive and fire resistant and require little maintenance. Stonework generally is more costly than brickwork. Figure 8.1 shows a cutaway of a brick-veneered exterior wall, the most common type of masonry material used on houses.

Refer to Figure 8.1 as you read. Starting with the inside of the wall is drywall (also called wallboard). Next is a vapor barrier made of paper, plastic or metal to keep moisture in the house from getting into the wall. Insulating material fills the space between the upright studs. Nailed to the outside of the studs is the sheathing—usually plywood sheets or insulating boards. Over the sheathing is sheathing paper to keep out wind and water. Flashing at the base of this paper carries off water from the wall, and weep holes between bricks allow water to escape. Finally, metal anchors tie the bricks to the frame wall.

FIGURE 8.1 Cutaway of Brick-Veneered Wall

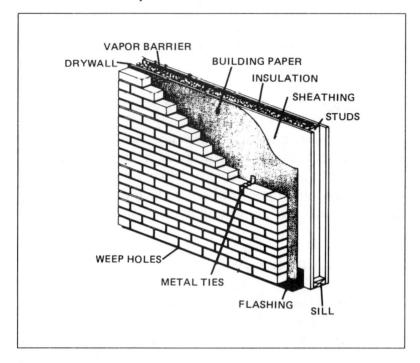

Solid brick and stone are seldom used today as structural walls because of the expense involved. They require extra-thick foundation walls, and craftspeople able to install them are scarce.

Stucco

Stucco is a type of mortar that lends itself to Spanish-inspired architecture. It is noted for its durability, insulation and resistance to fire, insects and mildew.

☞ **Money-$aving Tip #26** *The three most popular exterior wall choices are brick, wood siding and stucco. About half of all home shoppers prefer brick for exterior* *walls; about one-third prefer wood siding; and about one-fifth prefer stucco.*

Inspecting the Exterior Walls

Note the type (wood, stucco, masonry, aluminum, vinyl) and condition of the exterior walls. Check wood siding for bubbled or flaking paint, which may mean that the house has insufficient vapor-barrier protection. Probe wood siding for rot, especially the bottom boards along the foundation. Note bulges or cracks in stucco; deteriorating mortar between bricks or stones, as well as breakdown of the bricks; and dents, chips or cracks in aluminum or vinyl siding.

Check the trim around the doors and windows and at the corners of the house. It should be firmly in place and well caulked. There should be a tight seal where exterior walls meet chimney masonry.

Inspection Checklist

Exterior walls: wood clapboard/wood shingles/aluminum/
vinyl/brick veneer/stucco/other

Wood Siding

Yes No

___ ___ 1. Are all sections of siding firm?

___ ___ 2. Is the siding in good condition (no peeling paint or faded colors)?

___ ___ 3. Has siding been kept up so that there are no missing or decaying sections?

___ ___ 4. Is siding in good shape (no splits)?

____ ____   5. Do all joints fit tightly together (no open gaps) to prevent water penetration?

____ ____   6. Has the siding been nailed down properly?

____ ____   7. Is all sheathing concealed so that none shows between the boards?

Aluminum and Vinyl Siding

____ ____   8. Is the siding firm?

____ ____   9. Do all joints fit tightly together (no open gaps) to prevent water penetration?

____ ____   10. Is siding free of severe dents or scratches?

____ ____   11. Is siding in good shape (no cracked or missing sections)?

Brick

____ ____   12. Is the brick in good shape (no cracked, broken or missing bricks)?

____ ____   13. Is mortar in good shape (no signs of wear)?

____ ____   14. Are walls straight (no bows)?

Stucco

____ ____   15. Is the stucco surface free of settlement cracks, which would possibly indicate a problem in the structural wall?

____ ____   16. Are the walls straight (no bows)?

____ ____   17. Is the stucco firm (not pulling loose)?

____ ____   18. Is the surface in good shape (no evidence of patches)?

____ ____   19. Are the walls in good condition (no peeling paint or faded colors)?

Overall Rating

	Good	Fair	Poor
Exterior walls	—	—	—
Major Problems:			

Commonly Asked Questions

Q. Why do bricks have holes?

A. Bricks have holes to provide better adhesion with the mortar.

Q. What is clapboard *siding?*

A. Clapboard siding consists of wood pieces that are laid horizontally from the bottom of a house up to the top. The pieces overlap. The ends of individual pieces are butted together or to a corner or window or door trim.

Q. Based on home shoppers' preference, what are the top three exterior wall coverings for homes?

A. In order of preference, the top three alternatives are brick, wood and stucco.

Q. What are the biggest criticisms of aluminum siding?

A. It is easily dented, and the surface color can be scratched, exposing bare aluminum.

Q. Vinyl is a popular siding because it eliminates painting and reduces maintenance. Can vinyl also be used on the exterior wood trim?

A. Vinyl is not used for covering wood trim, but aluminum is. So, for a maintenance-free exterior, you can use vinyl for the siding and aluminum for the trim.

CHAPTER 9

Looking at Windows and Doors

Window styles do more than let the sunshine in. New window shapes—arches, circles, ovals and geometrics—along with the classic bays, bows, double-hung and casements, give exteriors a surprising facelift. Inside, they can make a room look bigger, brighter and create dramatic changes in the overall look of a room. The main parts of a window are shown in Figure 9.1.

A Window Primer

The most common window style is the *double-hung* (see Figure 9.2), which consists of upper and lower sashes that slide up or down using a pair of spring-lift mechanisms fastened to the sashes and jambs on either side. The *single-hung* is a variation of the double-hung, in that only the bottom sash moves. Weatherstripping along the jambs blocks air from seeping into living spaces. Double- and

FIGURE 9.1 Parts of a Window

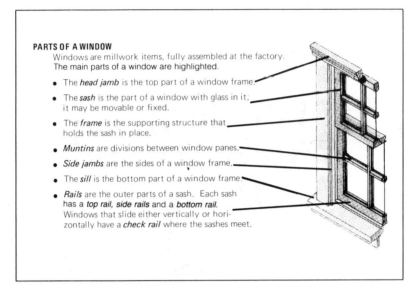

PARTS OF A WINDOW
Windows are millwork items, fully assembled at the factory. The main parts of a window are highlighted.

- The *head jamb* is the top part of a window frame.
- The *sash* is the part of a window with glass in it; it may be movable or fixed.
- The *frame* is the supporting structure that holds the sash in place.
- *Muntins* are divisions between window panes.
- *Side jambs* are the sides of a window frame.
- The *sill* is the bottom part of a window frame.
- *Rails* are the outer parts of a sash. Each sash has a *top rail*, *side rails* and a *bottom rail*. Windows that slide either vertically or horizontally have a *check rail* where the sashes meet.

single-hung windows are ideal for traditional architectural styles and require little maintenance.

The *casement* is another popular window choice. Casements are hinged at the side and open outward like a door. Unlike double-hungs, which require you to manually push the window up and down, casements are operated by turning a crank. Casement windows lock tightly, making them the best choice for stopping air infiltration. Because the sashes swing out, screens must be placed inside the window. Although they are more costly than double-hung windows, casements make an attractive alternative, especially for contemporary homes.

Awning windows operate much like casements except the sashes swing up rather than out. Awning windows are used primarily in basements or in attics or other tight spaces.

FIGURE 9.2 Window Types

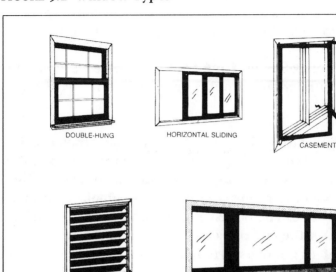

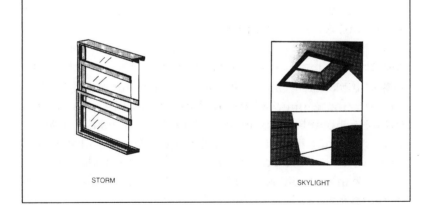

Horizontal sliders move back and forth on tracks, much like sliding patio doors. Like the double-hung type, only 50 percent of this window can be opened for fresh air.

Another primary style is the *fixed* window. As the name implies, this window is inoperative. With more of today's homes featuring oversized window walls, fixed or stationary windows are becoming more popular. Usually, stationary windows are mixed and matched with operative models to maximize light without limiting air flow.

☞ **Money-$aving Tip #27** *Money saved by purchasing cheap windows is offset by increases in heating and cooling costs.*

In addition to the basic window styles, an array of special shapes and sizes are available. For example, any standard door or window can be topped with a half-circle window or with a row of transoms. *Clerestories*–high-placed galleries of windows–can be placed underneath a home's overhangs or placed at the end of a cathedral ceiling to draw in extra light. And it's not unusual to find arched, round, elliptical or other shapes of windows that are mixed and matched to create a custom look.

Other types include bay or bow windows that add a traditional flair–and a little extra space and light–to a home.

Energy Savers

In the old days, one of the best ways to cut energy costs–and eliminate uncomfortable hot and cold spots–was to reduce a home's glass areas. Because of dramatic improvements in the thermal performance of glass, along with improved window construction techniques, today's homeowner can save energy without sacrificing natural light and expansive views.

A standard energy rating, called R-value, measures window efficiency. The higher the R-value, the better the thermal efficiency. Generally speaking, any windows rated R-3 or above are considered energy efficient and should perform well. You can find windows with ratings as high as R-5 to R-8.

High-efficiency ratings are achieved largely through the use of low-emissivity (low-E) glass. Low-E refers to a number of glazing strategies that significantly improve the energy performance of glass. These include building the windows with double or triple panes, filling the air pockets between the panes with argon gas, or using window films.

☞ **Money-$aving Tip #28** *A low-E coated, double-glass unit with gas fill, instead of standard double glazing, will improve the insulating value of the glass area by 40 to 50 percent.*

Window Frames

The material from which window frames are made plays a key role in determining the style and durability of the windows. There are four basic choices—wood, vinyl, fiberglass and aluminum.

Window frames made of wood are still viewed as the premium product. Wood frames are extremely attractive and stable, but they must be painted or stained for protection, so they require more maintenance than other window types.

Vinyl window frames have been gaining in popularity and respectability for new construction as well as for replacement. A cost-effective alternative to wood, vinyl frames tend to be solid, attractive and excellent at resisting heat and cold. Keep in mind, however, that vinyl frames cannot be painted. That means they offer low maintenance but limited color selection. Some vinyl frames are available with natural wood interior trim to improve their indoor appearance.

Fiberglass window frames are also growing in popularity because they cost less than wood. While fiberglass frames come in only a small selection of prefinished colors, they can easily be painted. As a result, you can take advantage of the low-maintenance finish on the exterior, but paint the interior window frames to match your decor.

☞ **Money-$aving Tip #29** *Both vinyl and fiberglass window frames are cost-effective alternatives to wood.*

Aluminum window frames are being used less today because they tend to transfer the cold indoors. They are also subject to pitting and other durability problems. The main advantage of aluminum window frames is their low cost, but they are adequate only in warm-weather climates.

Homeowners who want wood construction with a low-maintenance exterior can purchase wood windows clad with aluminum, vinyl or fiberglass. With clad windows, the interior frame can still be painted or stained to match your decor, but all exterior wood is sealed from the elements.

Window frames should be tight-fitting to minimize air leakage. Windows are giving you the message that they need attention when they become hard to operate or drafts are coming through. Even tiny cracks cause massive amounts of heating and cooling loss. A good test for a snug fit is to move a lighted candle around the window frame on a windy day. If the candle flickers, air is leaking through.

☞ **Money-$aving Tip #30** *Wood and vinyl window frames offer the best insulating value today.*

Noise Pollution

Windows can leak sound, just as pipes can leak water. Factors ranging from window design to installation technique affect the noise level in homes. In general, though, energy-efficient windows cut down on the amount of sound entering a home.

Doors

The style of an exterior door may initially attract your attention, but during an inspection, take time to consider all its features. An exterior door must be tight-fitting, weather-stripped to prevent air leaks, and able to offer security against intruders.

☞ **Money-$aving Tip #31** *Entrance doors that don't work properly are expensive to fix.*

Types of Exterior Doors

Exterior doors are available in solid wood (plank), veneer over solid wood, veneer over a hollow core, aluminum-clad wood, steel-clad wood, and steel or aluminum over a rigid-foam core. All but hollow-core exterior doors have insulating qualities. Hollow exterior doors are a sign of poor quality construction.

Wood doors require periodic painting. In addition, these doors are subject to chipping, cracking and shrinkage. Current manufacturers of wood doors, however, have developed techniques, such as impregnating the wood with plastic, that have almost eliminated these faults.

Aluminum and *steel* doors have a lighter inner core of wood, wood and foam, or rigid foam. The metal exterior comes primed or with a baked-enamel finish, is weather resistant and doesn't swell or shrink. It's also fire-retardant and, in some ways, more secure than its wood counterparts.

Fiberglass doors are made from a molded fiber skin, often with an etched wood-grain appearance, wrapped around an insulating urethane core and wood trim. Although it looks like wood when stained and painted, the fiberglass door has none of the warping and splitting problems of wood doors.

Sliding glass or *patio* doors have at least one fixed panel and one or more panels that slide in a wood or metal frame. They are preferred where view is desired.

The greatest energy loss is around the door rather than through it. Prehung entry systems, which include door, jamb, sill, weatherstripping and accessory components, tackle this problem.

Hardware, often purchased separately from the door unit, should be sturdy, not just good-looking. It's best to include a dead-bolt lock and keylocked knob-and-latch assembly for maximum security.

Interior Doors

Doors are made differently for exterior and interior use. Solid core doors are preferred for exterior doors because they provide better heat and sound insulation and are more resistant to warping. Hollow-core doors are used for interior locations, where heat and sound insulation are not as critical.

Inspecting the Windows and Doors

Open and shut all windows and doors to make sure they operate properly and seal tightly. Check for broken or cracked glass in windows. Make sure there are no holes in the screens. Check that both windows and doors are weatherstripped.

Look for discolored walls and buckled floorboards near windows. These are signs that water is leaking into the walls from around the windows. Cracks around the outside of the windows should be filled with caulking compound.

Inspection Checklist

Type of windows: double-hung/horizontal sliding/
                   casement/fixed/other
Storm windows: yes/no
Screens: yes/no
Window frames: wood/vinyl/fiberglass/aluminum/other
Exterior doors: wood/metal/fiberglass/sliding glass/
                   French/other

Yes   No

___   ___   1. Do all windows fit and operate easily?

___   ___   2. Do all doors open and close easily?

___   ___   3. Is the window glass in good shape (no cracked or broken windows)?

___   ___   4. Are window frames in good shape (not rotted or damaged in any way)?

___   ___   5. Are windows and doors free of water stains indicating leaks?

___   ___   6. Are the windows weatherstripped?

___   ___   7. Are all windows in good shape so they will not need replacing?

___   ___   8. Are window locks in good shape (not broken)?

___   ___   9. Are window frames in good condition (no peeling paint or faded colors)?

___   ___   10. Are all doors in good shape (not warped; no signs of rot)?

___   ___   11. Do the door locks operate properly?

___ ___   12. Is the framework that surrounds the doors clean and newly painted?

___ ___   13. Is the framework solid (not cracked)?

___ ___   14. Are the exterior doors weatherstripped?

___ ___   15. Are all doors in good condition (no peeling paint or faded colors)?

___ ___   16. Are all storm windows and doors weathertight?

Overall Rating

	Good	Fair	Poor
Windows	___	___	___
Doors	___	___	___
Major Problems:			

Commonly Asked Questions

Q. How can I find out about the sound qualities of my windows?

A. Most window manufacturers test their windows for sound control and will send you related data if you call their consumer inquiry department.

Q. Are there ways to tell the energy efficiency of windows?

A. Yes. Windows usually carry two energy-efficiency ratings. U-value measures how well heat flows through the window; the lower, the better. R-value measures resistance to heat passage; the higher, the better.

Q. *Are steel doors made of solid metal?*

A. No. They are made with a steel outer shell filled with insulating material.

Q. *What is a pocket door?*

A. A pocket door slides in and out of a slot built into the wall framing. It is used when there is little or no room to open a standard door.

CHAPTER 10

Evaluating Money-Saving Insulation

Insulation in a house helps homeowners economize on fuel and provides comfort in both warm and cold climates. It also reduces noise and blocks the spread of fire.

How Insulation Works

To understand how insulation works, it is important to know that heat flows naturally from a warmer to a cooler space. In the winter, this heat flow, or heat transfer, moves from all heated living spaces to adjacent unheated attics, garages and basements, or the outdoors; or through interior ceilings, walls and floors—wherever there is a difference in temperature. In the cooling season, the heat flow is often in the opposite direction, especially in air-conditioned houses. To maintain comfort, the heat lost must be replaced by your heating system and the heat gained must be removed by your air conditioner. Insulation of ceilings, walls and floors decreases this heat transfer by providing an effective resistance to the flow of heat.

Insulation isn't new. The pioneers stuffed walls with everything from straw to corn husks. Today, the most popular type of insulating material is fiberglass. What is new is the amount of insulation experts recommend for keeping a home comfortable in all seasons.

☞ **Money-$aving Tip #32** *The benefits of insulation—lower utility costs—continue for years.*

R-Values

The amount of insulation depends on the R-value needed and the space to be insulated. *R* means resistance to heat flow. The higher the R-value, the better its resistance.

The minimum R-value recommendations of the U.S. Department of Energy (DOE) are specific to zip code areas and take into account climate, heating and cooling needs, forms of heating used and energy prices. The guidelines cover insulation requirements for ceilings, floors, exterior walls, attics and crawl spaces.

The DOE estimates that 50 to 70 percent of the energy used in the average American home is for heating and cooling. Yet, most houses in the United States are not insulated to recommended levels.

In an insulation study, for example, it was found that the average insulation level in attics is about R-20. But the DOE now recommends an average of R-40.

As stated earlier, insulation helps retard heat flow in summer as well as winter. A properly insulated home can reduce summer cooling bills as well as winter heating bills. Because such a high percentage of the energy used in the average home goes for heating and cooling, adding insulation where needed is a practical, cost-effective step in conserving energy year round.

Nowhere is adding insulation more effective than in the attic. Because this space is usually accessible, adding insulation to the attic floor is the easiest way to improve the thermal performance of a home. In general, R-38 or R-40 insulation is recommended for most parts of the country, with even higher R-values economically justified by fuel savings in colder regions.

Insulation can serve the double purpose of heating and cooling a house. There are several areas in any house that should be insulated (see Figure 10.1). If attic space is not meant to be used as a living area, the floor of the attic is insulated; otherwise, the attic ceiling is insulated. All outside walls should be insulated, as should floors over unheated areas such as a crawl space. Insulation can be applied in the form of blankets or batts that are stapled between the studs, loose insulation that is blown into floor and wall spaces, or rigid fiberboard materials that are used structurally as sheathing or wallboard. A proper vapor barrier (also called vapor retarder) should be installed with any type of insulation. A vapor barrier is a waterproofing material that helps keep moisture from passing through the insulation and collecting inside walls, ceilings and floors. For example, when insulation is installed on an attic floor, there should be a vapor barrier on the floor between the insulation and the flooring.

Other Places To Insulate

Don't overlook two other areas in a home where energy can be saved—the hot water tank and the ductwork of the heating and air-conditioning system.

A hot water tank loses heat to the surrounding space. Wrapping insulation around the tank reduces this heat loss, which, in turn, reduces the energy needed to keep the water at the desired temperature. For a 40- to 50-gallon hot water tank, about 10 percent of the yearly cost for heating water can be saved this way.

☞ **Money-$aving Tip #33** *A well-insulated water heater reduces energy costs—particularly if it's located in an unheated area of the house.*

If water lines and the ducts of the heating and air-conditioning system run through unheated or uncooled spaces in the home, such as attic or crawl spaces, then the water lines and the ducts should be insulated.

☞ **Money-$aving Tip #34** *Make sure the ducts in the air-conditioning system are properly sealed and insulated, especially those that pass through the attic or other uncooled spaces.*

Checking for Insulation

Most older homes were built when energy was abundant and cheap, and may have little or no insulation or the amount of insulation is not adequate by today's standards. Look at Figure 10.1, which shows the four areas where home insulation is required. These are the areas you should check first.

Normally you can see insulation on the attic floor. It is more difficult to inspect exterior walls. One method is to use an electrical outlet on the wall. But first, be sure to turn off the power to the outlet. Then remove the coverplate and shine a flashlight into the opening to see if there is insulation in the wall. Check for insulation in unfinished basement ceilings and walls, above crawl spaces and in walls between an unheated garage and living space.

FIGURE 10.1 Areas That Require Insulation

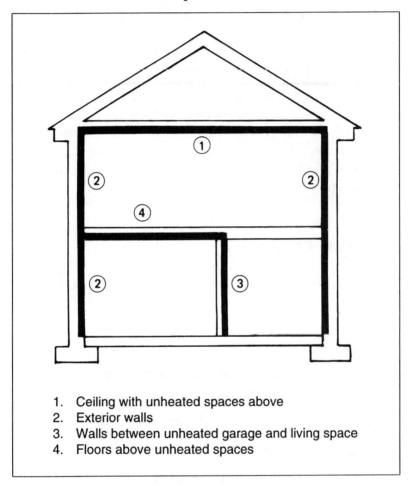

1. Ceiling with unheated spaces above
2. Exterior walls
3. Walls between unheated garage and living space
4. Floors above unheated spaces

If you do not know the R-value of the insulation in the house, or whether it meets the requirements in the area, call the local electric or gas company to set up a free or low-cost energy audit.

How the Agent Can Help

No matter how you heat or cool a home, you can reduce the load on the heating and cooling equipment with the proper amount and placement of insulation. Whether a home needs additional insulation will depend on the climate in which the house is located and the amount of insulation, if any, it already has. For guidance, ask your real estate agent for information on insulation requirements for your area.

Inspection Checklist

Types of insulation: batts or blanket/loose fill/rigid board/ other

R-value: floors _____ walls _____ ceiling _____

Yes   No

____ ____ 1. Has an energy audit been done on the house?

____ ____   If so, were the results positive?

____ ____ 2. Are the basement walls fully insulated?

____ ____ 3. Is the attic adequately insulated?

____ ____ 4. Are unheated areas such as garages and crawl spaces insulated?

____ ____ 5. Are the exterior perimeter walls insulated?

____ ____ 6. Does the house have good-quality wall and ceiling insulation?

____ ____ 7. Do the insulation materials have vapor barriers?

___ ___   8. Is the house free of asbestos insulation?

___ ___   9. Is the house free of formaldehyde insulation?

Overall Rating   **Good Fair Poor**

Insulation   ___   ___   ___
Major Problems:

Commonly Asked Questions

Q. Does R-value refer to thickness?

A. R-value refers to a material's resistance to heat flow, not thickness. Different types of insulation with the same thickness may have different R-values, and vice versa. Tiny air pockets trapped in insulating material resist the passage of heat—heat gain in warmer months and heat loss in colder months. The higher the insulation's R-value, the greater the insulating power.

Q. What are the leading causes of energy waste in most homes?

A. Air leakage, moisture infiltration and inadequate insulation.

Q. How does moisture in a house affect insulation?

A. The warm air inside a house contains water vapor. If this vapor passes into the insulation and condenses, it can cause significant loss of insulating value.

Q. *What does a vapor barrier do for insulation?*

A. A vapor barrier helps keep moisture from passing through the insulation and collecting inside walls, ceilings and floors.

Q. *Does insulation protect against hot temperatures as well as cold?*

A. Yes. Regardless of inside or outside temperatures, the main concern is heat. Insulation helps retard the process of summer heat entering the home. In winter, insulation helps keep the house warm by reducing the escape of interior heat.

CHAPTER 11

Testing the Mechanical Systems

A thorough home inspection should include an examination of the heating, cooling, plumbing and electrical systems for problems.

Plumbing

Plumbing basically consists of pipes that bring fresh water into the house, fixtures that control water once it is there and pipes that drain waste water out of a house.

Water Pipes

In many areas, copper is the only acceptable material for water pipes. Brass has been used for many years, but now it is expensive. Polybutalene plastic is the newest material used for pipes. It is gaining in popularity among builders, although its use is still not permitted in many areas.

Plumbing is often a problem in older homes with iron or steel pipes. Lead piping is considered a health hazard—it has been tied to impaired mental ability—and must be changed if found in the house.

Fixtures

Toilets, bathtubs and sinks are made of vitreous china, enameled cast iron, enameled steel, stainless steel or plastic. Plumbing fixtures have relatively long lives and are often replaced because of their obsolete style long before they have worn out.

☞ **Money-$aving Tip #35** *To reduce water bills, look for water-saving toilets that use less than five gallons for flushing. Nearly 10 gallons of water goes down the drain every time a standard toilet is flushed.*

Inspecting the Plumbing

Assess all the plumbing. For a quick check, open all faucets and flush all toilets. Check the water pressure while you observe how fast the water drains. If you find a stopped-up drain, you can pinpoint the location of the clog. If only one fixture doesn't drain, the blockage is near that fixture. If two or more fixtures are clogged, something is lodged in the main drain. If no drains work, the blockage is near or in the sewer drain itself.

Check to see if any faucets drip when they have been turned off. If so, the washers or valves, or both, need replacing.

Check the insides of sink cabinets for moisture. Inspect the nuts on faucets and supply tubes to make sure they are tight.

Listen for sounds in the piping system when you turn on the faucets. This could mean trouble. Vibrations in the pipes can loosen fittings, causing leaks to occur.

Does each toilet have a separate shutoff valve? This allows you to cut off water to the toilet without having to turn the water off in the entire house. Sinks should also have shutoff valves for the same reason.

Improper venting is a defect often found in plumbing systems. If you hear sucking or gurgling noises after a fixture is drained, or smell a foul odor, most likely sewer gas, coming from the fixture, chances are the fixture does not have a vent pipe extending to the outside.

Check the floor around the toilet. Is there any sign of water damage? If so, it was probably caused by a broken toilet seal.

Check for water leaks in pipes. Although most of the plumbing is hidden between walls or under floors, check any exposed pipes in the basement or crawl space for signs of leaks, corrosion or recent repair jobs.

Water Heater

A water heater is basically an insulated metal tank that does just what its name implies.

Check the water heater for the following:

- *Age.* Because water heaters run continuously, they have the shortest life span (10-12 years) of any major appliance.
- *Size.* The size needed will depend on several factors including the number of people in the family, the hot water consumption during peak use periods (such as bathing or laundering) and the recovery time required by the tank. Manufacturers recommend that the tank be placed closest to the point of use. Most families require a 40- to 50-gallon tank.

- *Safety features.* Most water heaters have a pressure-relief valve to prevent explosions, if the heater continues to heat beyond the predetermined temperature.
- *Leaks.* Check the water heater for signs of rust and leakage.

☞ **Money-$aving Tip #36** *Few things in a house are as expensive to repair as plumbing. So check the system carefully.*

Inspection Checklist

Plumbing Information

Water pipes: copper/galvanized metal/polybutalene plastic/other
Drain lines: cast iron/plastic/other
Water heater: gas/electric/oil
  Gallon capacity: _____
  Age: _____

Yes No

_____ _____   1. Check all exposed water pipes. Are they free of any signs of leaks, corrosion or deterioration in the water lines or their fittings?

_____ _____   2. Are all drain lines clear, with no signs of deterioration?

_____ _____   3. Are the pipes insulated?

_____ _____   4. Is the basement free of any signs of sewage backup?

_____ _____   5. Check the faucets for operation. Is there sufficient water pressure at each faucet?

____ ____   6. Is the water clear (no rusty water coming from any faucet)?

____ ____   7. Are faucets in good shape (no drips)?

____ ____   8. Check all sinks in the house. Do they drain properly?

____ ____   9. Check under the sink. Is this area free of signs of leaks or water damage?

____ ____   10. Are countertops in good shape (no need for repair or replacement)?

____ ____   11. Do the water pipes have shutoff valves in the basement?

____ ____   In the kitchen?

____ ____   In the bathrooms?

____ ____   12. Do plumbing fixtures have proper venting?

____ ____   13. Is there sufficient storage in the bathrooms?

____ ____   14. Are there quality fixtures?

____ ____   15. Are there sufficient electrical outlets in the bathrooms?

____ ____   16. Flush each toilet. Does each one operate properly?

____ ____   17. Does each toilet have a water shutoff valve?

____ ____   18. Do all of the toilets flush quietly? (Make sure they're not excessively noisy.)

____ ____   19. After the toilet has been flushed and filled, does it stop running?

____ ____ 20. Look at the floor around the toilets. Is it free of water damage?

____ ____ 21. Look carefully at the ceilings beneath the bathrooms. Are they free of water stains?

____ ____ 22. Do the tubs and showers drain properly?

____ ____ 23. Do the tubs and sinks hold water without seepage?

____ ____ 24. Check the walls around the tubs and/or showers. Are they free of water damage?

____ ____ 25. Are tiles in good shape (not cracked or missing)?

____ ____ 26. Check the gallon capacity of the water heater. Does it meet your family's needs?

____ ____ 27. Is the water heater in good shape? (Check its age and for signs of rust and water leaks.)

____ ____ 28. If the house has a septic tank, is it free of strong odors coming from the tank area?

____ ____ 29. Is the septic tank area free of standing water?

____ ____ 30. Is the tank cover accessible?

____ ____ 31. Does the septic system work well? (Ask the owner how often the holding tank has been pumped out over the past several years. A septic system is very costly to replace.)

____ ____ 32. If there is a well, does it work efficiently? (Ask the owner.)

Overall Rating

	Good	Fair	Poor
Overall plumbing system	___	___	___
Drainage/plumbing	___	___	___
Water pressure	___	___	___
Water heater	___	___	___
Septic system	___	___	___
Well	___	___	___
Plumbing fixtures	___	___	___

Major Problems:

Heating and Cooling

The heating and cooling system is the heart of the comfortable house. At a minimum, you want to know what kind of heating and cooling system is in place, what condition it is in and how much it will cost to operate.

Heating

The most common heating systems include the following:

- *Forced warm air.* This is the most common type of heating system. A furnace heats air, and a blower sends the hot air through the house. Return vents and pipes bring the cool air back to the furnace. Each furnace has a capacity rated in British Thermal Units (BTUs). The number of BTUs given represents the furnace's heat output from either gas, oil or electric firing.
- *Steam.* This kind of system is usually found in older homes. A furnace heats water until steam forms. The steam circulates through pipes into radiators in the rooms. As steam cools, it turns back into water, which then returns to the furnace.

- *Hot water.* This system works like steam heat, but instead of circulating steam, it circulates hot water that heats the rooms.
- *Baseboard/electric.* This system uses heated elements placed along the baseboards of walls.
- *Radiant.* This type of system was common in houses built in the 1950s and 1960s. It uses pipes built into the floor to heat the rooms. Radiant heating limits what can be placed on the floor. Thick rugs, for example, will absorb much of the heat that would otherwise warm the room.

Air-Conditioning

Almost all new homes today are centrally air-conditioned. Air-conditioning units are rated either in BTUs or in tons. Twelve thousand BTUs are the equivalent of a one-ton capacity.

The efficiency of an air-conditioning system is rated on a scale called the *Seasonal Energy Efficiency Ratio (SEER).* The SEER is a relative measure of how much cooling you get from the electricity the unit uses. SEERs range from a low of about 6 (typical for existing equipment) to a high of around 14.

An air-conditioning unit with a SEER of 12 will use half of the electricity of a unit with a SEER of six. The wider the difference between the SEER ratings, the greater the savings.

Combination heating and cooling systems are common in new homes. The most prevalent is the conventional warm-air heating system with a cooling unit attached. The same ducts and blower that force warm air are used to force cool air.

FIGURE 11.1 Heat Pump Operation During Heating and
Cooling Cycles

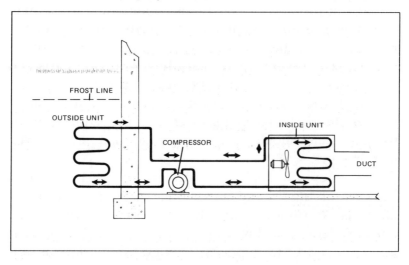

Heat Pump

Many experts believe the heat pump eventually will
replace today's conventional combination heating and
cooling systems.

A heat pump (see Figure 11.1), like a refrigerator,
depends on the fact that gases give off heat when liquefied
by pressure. Gas is brought in from *outside coils* to a *heavy-
duty compressor.* When sufficient pressure is added, the liquefied gas heats the *indoor coils,* which in turn feed heat to
the *air-duct system.* Back outside and with the pressure off,
the chilled gas picks up more outdoor heat. The cycle is
reversed to cool the house in summer.

🖙 **Money-$aving Tip #37** *Be sure that all supply
ducts are well insulated and that cracks are taped to prevent air leaks.*

High-Efficiency Air Conditioners

Many of the newest central air conditioners use a quiet and efficient scroll compressor. The scroll compressor has revolutionized the heating and air-conditioning business over the last several years. With fewer moving parts and higher efficiency than conventional piston compressors, the scroll adds real value to heat-pump and air-conditioning systems. In addition to saving electricity, the scroll is quieter to operate and should have a longer life than piston-driven compressors.

Other new high-efficiency designs use variable-speed compressor, blower and fan motors. The internal electronic controls continuously match the cooling output to the cooling needs of the house. Since these air conditioners run longer at the slower speeds, temperature variations and blower noise are not as noticeable between on/off cycles.

On mild days, the air conditioner runs more slowly and on very hot days it runs faster. Not only is electricity saved by varying the cooling output, but the humidity level inside the home is also better controlled.

The variable-speed blower and fan motor are also extra efficient.

Room Air Conditioners

In areas where the number of hot, humid days doesn't warrant the cost of installing central air-conditioning, room air conditioners provide low-cost summer comfort. Although a room air conditioner can be placed in a window, it's better to frame it into an exterior wall below the window, just above floor level. This way, the window can still provide light and ventilation.

☞ **Money-$aving Tip #38** *Don't set your thermostat at a colder setting than normal when you turn on your air* *conditioner. It will* not *cool faster. It* will *cool to a lower temperature than you need and use more energy.*

Inspecting the Heating and Air-Conditioning System

Technical aspects of heating and air-conditioning should be handled by an experienced and qualified person. As a home shopper, all you can really do is check that the system is working and that it adequately heats and cools the house.

Operate the heating and cooling system. Get an idea of how quickly the system responds, how evenly it seems to heat or cool, how forcefully the air comes out of the vents and its relative temperature. If the system is not heating or cooling properly, it should be checked by an expert.

☞ **Money-$aving Tip #39** *There have been many significant improvements in the design of heating and cooling systems. A high-efficiency model can cut your heating and air-conditioning costs in half.*

Inspection Checklist

Heating and Air-Conditioning

Type of heating system:	central forced air/hot water/heat pump/other
Type of air-conditioning system:	central forced air/heat pump/room AC/other
Fuel:	gas/electric/oil
Age of equipment: _____	

Yes   No

___   ___   1. Does the heating and air-conditioning equipment use the least expensive fuel for the area?

     ____ ____   2. Does the house have energy-efficient heating and cooling equipment?

____ ____   3. Are the present utility bills acceptable for your budget?

____ ____   4. Do all rooms have air vents (or radiators)?

____ ____   5. Are the vent openings adjustable?

____ ____   6. Are the vents in the house clean and equipped with filtering devices?

____ ____   7. If the house uses a hot water system, are radiators and piping free of leaks?

____ ____   8. Is sufficient warm (or cold) air reaching all rooms through the vents (or radiators)?

____ ____   9. Has the gas or oil furnace had an annual checkup?

____ ____   10. Is the Freon line in the central air unit free of leaks or other problems?

____ ____   11. Do all ducts have dampers?

____ ____   12. Look at the joints connecting individual ducts. Are they properly sealed (no open gaps through which air is leaking)?

____ ____   13. Are the ducts (or pipes) wrapped with insulation?

____ ____   14. Is the heating and cooling equipment relatively new? (Check to see if they will need to be replaced soon due to age.)

____ ____   15. Does the equipment appear to be in good shape (no rust, dents, holes, etc.)?

____ ____   16. Is the condensation line for the air conditioner clear?

____ ____ 17. Is the thermostat properly located (away from vents or ducts, etc., that may influence the temperature reading, causing the system to cycle on and off more than normal)?

____ ____ 18. Is the size of the heating and cooling unit adequate for the number of square feet in the house?

In a Gas-Fired Heating System

____ ____ 19. Is the unit free of gas odors?

____ ____ 20. Are gas pipes free of any rust or corrosion?

____ ____ 21. Is there a gas alarm for the house?

Overall Rating	Good	Fair	Poor
Heating system	____	____	____
Air-conditioning system	____	____	____
Average dollar amount of gas bills	____	____	____
Average dollar amount of oil bills	____	____	____
Major Problems:			

Working with Electricity

A home electrical system consists of electrical boxes, wiring, breakers, switches and receptacles.

A good residential electrical system must have three important characteristics. First, it must meet all National Electrical Code (NEC) safety requirements—each major appliance should have its own circuit, and lighting circuits should be isolated from electrical equipment that causes fluctuations in voltage. Second, the system must meet the home's existing needs and must have the capacity to accommodate room additions and new appliances. Finally, it should be convenient; there should be enough switches,

FIGURE 11.2 Breaker-Type Service Panel

lights and outlets located so that occupants will not have to walk in the dark or use extension cords.

Electrical service from the power company is brought into the home through the transformer and the meter into a *circuit breaker box* (or a *fuse panel* in older homes). The circuit breaker box (see Figure 11.2) is the distribution panel for the many electrical circuits in the house. In case of a power overload, the heat generated by the additional flow of electrical power will cause the circuit breaker to open at the breaker box, thus reducing the possibility of electrical fires. The architect or the builder is responsible for adhering to local building codes, which regulate electrical wiring. All electrical installations are inspected by the local building authorities, which assures the homeowner of the system's compliance with the building codes.

Residential wiring circuits are rated by the voltage that they are designed to carry. In the past, most residences were wired only for 110-volt capacity. Today, because of the many built-in appliances in use, 220-volt to 240-volt service is generally necessary. *Amperage,* the strength of a current expressed in amperes, is shown on the circuit breaker panel. The circuit breaker panel (or fuse panel) should have a capacity of at least 100 amperes. A larger service (150 to 200 or more amperes) may be needed if there is electric heat or an electric range or if the house has more than 3,000 square feet. New wiring will be required if the existing board's capacity is only 30 to 60 amperes. If there are fewer than eight or ten circuits, it probably will be necessary to add more. Each circuit is represented by a separate circuit breaker or fuse. A house with a lot of electrical equipment may require 15 to 20 or more circuits.

☞ **Money-$aving Tip #40** *Be sure there are enough electrical circuits now to meet future needs and avoid costly changes later.*

Inadequate electrical systems are the most common and most dangerous problems found when inspecting older homes.

No matter how skilled you are, you must be wary about checking parts of the electrical system. Electricity is not only dangerous if you do not know what you are doing, but working with it is often forbidden by local or national codes.

If you plan to work with electricity, here are some safety measures to keep you from getting shocked.

- Before you begin working on any electrical line, be sure to halt the flow of electricity going through it. This means removing the fuse that controls that circuit or, if the house has circuit breakers, pushing the breaker to the *off* position.

- No matter what you are doing, even removing a fuse or shutting off a circuit breaker, never stand on a damp floor.
- Do not use an aluminum ladder, especially near entrance wires.
- Don't touch anything that can be a ground for electricity, such as a water or gas pipe.
- Remove a plug from an outlet by pulling outward on the plug, not by holding on to the wire and tugging.
- Do not use a radio or any other electric appliance in the bathroom or near a sink or tub or wherever there is water.

Inspecting the Electrical System

Check the electrical service panel to determine whether fuses or circuit breakers are used, and whether the capacity is sufficient to handle the present and future needs of the house. The minimum capacity recommended for most houses today is a 3-wire, 240-volt, 100-ampere service. Service of 150 to 200 or more amperes is needed to power electrical heating and air-conditioning or for larger homes. The amperage is usually stamped on the main circuit breaker, or somewhere else on the box. Systems with only 30-amperes are now obsolete and houses with 60 amperes in capacity normally sell for less than similar homes with greater electrical service.

Open the main electrical box cover and look at the breakers or fuses. There should be at least 10 to 15 separate circuits—more in a house with a lot of electrical equipment.

Pull the main disconnect switch. Does it shut off all electrical circuits? If not, a serious defect may exist in the system. The electrical system may be a maze of added-on circuits. If the house has not been rewired in the past 30 years, it may need an extensive electrical overhaul, which is expensive.

Do circuit breakers or fuses trip or blow regularly? This is always a sign of trouble if it happens consistently, and the cause should be determined and corrected.

Does the home have copper or aluminum wires? Copper wire is best. Aluminum heats up much more quickly than copper and is not as good a conductor of electricity. Because it has been linked to increased residential fires, you should be wary of buying a house that has 100 percent aluminum wiring. Copper-clad aluminum wire (aluminum wire with a thin coating of copper) does not appear to have the problems associated with 100 percent aluminum wire.

☞ **Money-$aving Tip #41** *Be sure the wiring in the house meets code standards and is safe.*

Check the number of electrical outlets in the living areas of the house—particularly in the kitchen. Code requirements usually indicate that for every 12 linear feet of wall, there should be at least one double receptacle. In some areas of the house, such as the kitchen, you might want outlets as close as six feet or less. Are there enough light switches throughout the house? At a minimum, light switches should be beside every doorway into a room.

Caution

Do not touch any exposed wiring or probe with tools in electrical panels. Electricity is technical, complicated and dangerous.

☞ **Money-$aving Tip #42** *Don't use more light than you need. About 15 percent of the electricity we use in our homes goes into lighting.*

Inspection Checklist

Electrical Information

Ampere service capacity: _____
Number of circuits: _____
Wires: copper/copper-clad aluminum/ aluminum

Yes No

___ ___   1. Do the living areas of the house have electrical outlets?

___ ___   2. Are all outlets in good working condition?

___ ___   3. Are all switches and outlets properly grounded?

___ ___   4. Are there outside electrical outlets?

___ ___   Do they work?

___ ___   5. Are the covers over outdoor outlets weathertight?

___ ___   6. Are all outlets three-holed? (The third hole is the grounding connection.)

___ ___   7. Are all switches and outlets in good shape?

___ ___   8. Do appliances have their own separate circuits?

___ ___   9. Is there a main disconnect switch?

___ ___   10. Pull the main disconnect switch. Does it shut off all electrical circuits? (If not, a serious defect exists in the system.)

___ ___   11. Are there enough circuits to serve your needs?

___ ___   12. Does the wiring meet the code?

___   ___   13. Has copper or copper-clad aluminum wiring been used throughout the house instead of 100 percent aluminum?

___   ___   14. Are all light fixtures working?

___   ___   15. Are all circuit breakers working?

___   ___   16. Are all fuses or circuit breakers cool to the touch? (If they are warm, a serious defect may exist in the system.)

Overall Rating	**Good**	**Fair**	**Poor**
Wiring	___	___	___
Ampere service capacity	___	___	___
Number of circuits	___	___	___
Number of electrical outlets per room	___	___	___
Number of light switches per room	___	___	___
Average dollar amount of electric bills	___	___	___

Major Problems:

How *the Agent Can Help*

You can't always uncover everything during your inspection. For example, you aren't going to crack open a wall and check the wiring. Or, if it's winter and the heat is running, it may not be possible to test the effectiveness of the air-conditioning system throughout the house. In cases like these, you may want your agent to get a written statement from the seller indicating that the mechanical systems in the house are in good working order.

Commonly Asked Questions

Q. What is meant by zoned heating and cooling systems?

A. Zoning simply means heating (or cooling) different spaces according to need. This is accomplished by dividing a house into two, three or even four zones—each controlled by a separate thermostat. Warm or cool air is delivered only to those rooms where it's needed and when it's needed.

Q. Is an annual service contract for the home's heating and cooling system a prudent investment?

A. If you aren't willing or able to perform simple periodic maintenance, such as changing the air filter or lubricating a blower motor, a contract for service is advisable.

Q. Can installing a new furnace affect a home's ventilation needs?

A. Anytime you change a home's heating and cooling equipment or make weatherization improvements that tighten a house, ventilation needs should be reassessed. In many cases, contractors should add new ventilation when they install a new furnace or boiler. In all cases, the homeowner should be advised that humidity problems may occur and that it may be necessary to add ventilation at a later date.

Q. When should I invest in a new heating and cooling system?

A. If your furnace or boiler is more than 20 years old, if your heat pump is more than 10, or if your system was oversized to begin with (a very common practice), it probably would be worth investing in a new high-efficiency system. Certainly you should consider new equipment before making any significant repairs to the old unit.

Q. Is it good practice to oversize heating and cooling systems?

A. No. Instead of doing the heat-loss and heat-gain calculations necessary to properly size the system, many dealers oversize the equipment by 10, 20 or even 30 percent as a "fudge factor." Since oversized heating and cooling systems cycle on and off too frequently, they end up being costly, uncomfortable and noisy. Some experts believe it's actually better to slightly undersize the system.

CHAPTER 12

Floors and Floor Coverings

For years, floor coverings were simply walked on. Today, they command more respect. Serving much more than a practical purpose, floorings have become fashionable.

Flooring falls into two basic categories: hard and soft. The first group runs the gamut from basic concrete to elegant marble and includes wood, ceramic tile, slate, stone and brick. In the second group are carpets, area rugs and resilient flooring, such as cork or cushioned vinyl.

Hard Flooring

Wood Floors

Wood floors were the traditional choice from 1885, when machinery to cut tongue-and-groove joints was introduced, until the mid-1960s when the Federal Housing Administration approved the inclusion of wall-to-wall carpeting in home mortgages.

Using wood has several advantages. Wood acts as a natural insulator. It would take 15 inches of concrete to equal the insulation value of 1 inch of hardwood. In addition, wood flooring enhances a home's value. A national survey of real estate agents concluded that people perceive that hardwood flooring means quality. And the improvement of sealers and finishes has minimized the care of wood floors and increased their durability.

☞ **Money-$aving Tip #43** *Wood floors suggest warmth, quality and good taste and are an asset when it comes time to sell a house.*

Ceramic Tile

Ceramic tile remains traditional for bathroom floors. It also often is used as a floor covering for kitchens and entryways. Ceramic tile holds a commanding position for its long-and-hard-wearing qualities and the ease with which it's cleaned.

Other Hard Flooring

Brick, stone, slate, terrazzo and marble make beautiful flooring materials and are most practical for entryways, bathrooms, family rooms and perhaps kitchens.

Soft Flooring

Carpeting

On cold winter days, wall-to-wall carpeting provides a warm surface for bare feet. Quiet is preserved by carpeting's ability to absorb as much as ten times the noise other flooring materials do. Combined with the aesthetic benefits of carpeting's various colors, textures and styles, it's easy to see why carpeting covers 70 percent of all floors in America.

A rule of thumb in carpet quality is that the denser the carpet, the better quality it is. To determine its density, roll back a corner of the carpet and see how much of the backing shows through the pile. The more backing you see, the less dense the carpet is.

Resilient Flooring

Resilient flooring is a term used for sheets or squares of synthetic floor-covering materials. Linoleum was the first resilient flooring, followed by asphalt tiles and then vinyl flooring. Resilient flooring is manufactured in both sheet and tile form.

Checking the Flooring

Wood remains one of the most popular of flooring surfaces. A quick look at the condition of the wood will tell you much. If there is evidence of decay or weakness, a new floor may have to be laid. A floor that squeaks when you walk on it is not necessarily bad, but it may indicate workmanship and quality that is less than perfect.

To inspect the structural integrity of the flooring system, jump in the center of rooms. Springy floors may indicate sagging joints and beams, which are expensive to reinforce.

In rooms with wall-to-wall carpeting, check to see if it is worn and in need of replacement. New carpeting is expensive. But even if the carpeting is in good shape, can you stand living with it? See if you can lift up an edge of the carpeting and get a look at the actual condition of the floor below. If there's a good hardwood surface underneath, you can always get rid of the carpet. If it's made of plywood or pine boards, you'll have to stick with the existing carpet, buy new carpet or install a finished floor.

On tile floors, check to see if any are scratched, loose or broken. Loose tiles often indicate moisture problems.

Inspection Checklist

Floor Covering

Kitchen: vinyl tile/linoleum/wood/carpeting/ceramic tile/other

Bathrooms: ceramic tile/vinyl tile/linoleum/carpeting/ other

Living room: carpeting/wood/vinyl tile/linoleum/other

Family room: carpeting/wood/vinyl tile/linoleum/brick/ other

Bedrooms: carpeting/wood/vinyl tile/linoleum/other

Entryway: wood/vinyl tile/ceramic tile/slate/carpeting/ other

Hallways: carpeting/wood/vinyl tile/ceramic tile/other

Wood Flooring

Yes   No

___   ___   1. Are the floors finished and sealed correctly?

___   ___   2. Is the floor finish in good shape?

___   ___   3. Are floors free of squeaks? (A squeak may simply indicate a need to be renailed, but may also be part of a more serious structural problem.)

___ ___   4. Is the floor firm? (An unusual spring to the floor as you walk across it could indicate a subfloor problem.)

___ ___   5. Is flooring in good shape? (Make sure there is no rotting, which usually occurs at bathrooms or door thresholds.)

Resilient Flooring

___ ___   6. Is the linoleum or tile smooth? (Bumps or hollows indicate the subfloor wasn't properly prepared.)

___ ___   7. Is the surface of the linoleum free of cracks, tears or noticeable marks? (If not, the only correction is total replacement of the flooring.)

___ ___   8. Are individual tiles in good shape? (If not, these can be individually replaced.)

Hard Tile Flooring

___ ___   9. Are tiles in good shape (no cracked, loose, or missing tiles)? (Several cracked tiles could be the result of house settlement, perhaps indicating a serious structural problem.)

___ ___   10. Is grout firmly in place?

___ ___   11. Is the flooring level? (High or low spots could pose a safety hazard.)

___ ___   12. Is this type of flooring—particularly brick, slate and marble—in areas that do not receive a lot of water? (These materials are slippery when wet.)

Wall-to-Wall Carpeting

_____ _____   13. Are there good quality carpets in the house? (In general, the tighter the twist of the yarn, and the closer together the individual tufts in a row, the better quality the carpet is. In shags, however, density is not an important factor.)

_____ _____   14. Is there good quality padding underneath the carpets?

_____ _____   15. Are the carpets in good condition?

_____ _____   16. Are the carpets tightly stretched? (Any looseness will cause the carpet to wear much faster.)

_____ _____   17. Is the carpet free of worn or torn spots?

_____ _____   18. Are seams inconspicuous?

_____ _____   19. Is the carpet free of stains?

_____ _____   20. Are all carpets relatively clean? (Cleaning may not help excessively dirty carpeting.)

Overall Rating   Good Fair Poor

Wood flooring   ___   ___   ___
Resilient flooring   ___   ___   ___
Hard tile flooring   ___   ___   ___
Wall-to-wall carpeting   ___   ___   ___
Major Problems:

Commonly Asked Questions

Q. What causes floors to squeak?

A. A section of floor has separated from an uneven joist below. So, whenever you step on that spot, the floor squeaks as it rubs against the nail.

Q. Are floor squeaks serious?

A. Minor squeaks are not serious. But when other symptoms are present, such as sagging and sloping floors, the problem might be structural. The floor joists might be too small or lack support from adequate bridging, causing the sagging or sloping. Excessive settlement of the house or defective framing can also cause floors to slope or sag.

Q. Will thick padding make a carpet last longer?

A. Thick, soft padding may make a carpet feel luxurious, but often will wear the carpet faster because it lets the backing flex too much.

CHAPTER 13

Interior Wall Coverings, Ceilings and Trim

Most interior walls of a house are made of wood studs covered with gypsum wallboard, prefinished paneling or solid wood paneling. Plaster walls were once popular, but they are used less frequently today.

Interior Walls and Finishing

Interior walls are the partitioning dividers for individual rooms and are usually covered with *gypsum wallboard,* although plaster is sometimes used. The terms *drywall* and *plasterboard* are synonymous with wallboard. Wallboard is finished by a process known as *taping* and *floating.* Taping covers the joints between the sheets of wallboard. Floating is the process of smoothing out the walls by applying a plaster texture over the joints and rough edges where nails attach the wallboard to the wall studs. *Fiberboard* is an

143

alternative to wallboard, although it is more expensive. It is made from gypsum ore and recycled paper, mainly newsprint. Fiberboard is stronger, easier to install, more fire resistant, and controls sound and moisture better than wallboard.

Wall finishing is one of the most important decorator items in the home. Paint and wallpaper should be selected for both beauty and utility. Paneling is often used in less formal rooms and should be installed over a base of finished or unfinished wallboard to improve the insulation and soundproof values of the walls. Either ceramic or plastic tiles are used extensively as bathroom wall coverings.

☞ **Money-$aving Tip #44** *Most home shoppers prefer a combination of ceramic tile and vinyl wallpaper as a covering for bathroom walls, creating a positive effect on the house's resale value. Ceramic tile is usually installed wherever water comes in contact with the wall.*

Ceilings

In homes with gypsum wallboard, ceilings are often made of the same material and need no further decorating treatment except paint.

Trim

Trim work covers the seams between walls and adjoining structures (ceilings, door and window frames, and floors) and at the same time gives a finished decorator touch to a room. Trim, which is made of wood, hardboard or vinyl, should be selected in a style that is complementary to the overall decor of the house.

In the past, architects often designed unique trim work (also called *moldings*) for homes. But today, trim work comes in standard sizes and shapes and its use is decreasing. Simple baseboards are used in most homes to protect the walls from damage due to cleaning equipment or furniture.

Inspecting the Interior Walls, Ceilings and Trim

Check walls and ceilings in all rooms, including closets and stairways, for stains, falling plaster and peeling paint. These symptoms indicate moisture damage.

Inspect room ceilings under bathrooms for water stains caused by deteriorated toilet gaskets. A faulty gasket allows water to seep between finished flooring and subflooring.

Check painted walls or ceilings for cracks or bulges. Hairline cracks are not serious. They can be filled in with spackling paste and repainted. However, larger cracks or bulges may indicate serious structural problems.

Check the condition of wallpaper to see that it is not curled at the edges or faded. Make sure all paneling is securely fastened and in good condition. Sometimes wallpaper or paneling could be hiding faults in the wall itself. If you notice some discoloration or an uneven surface, find out the cause.

Check the tub or shower walls in the bathrooms for cracked or missing tiles and loose or missing grout. Eventually, water seeping behind the tile will cause damage to the subsurface.

Make sure all trim and molding is in place. Check for missing, cracked or broken sections, as well as poor workmanship.

Inspection Checklist

Types of Walls and Ceilings

Interior walls: wallboard/plaster/wood/wallpaper/other
Ceilings: wallboard/plaster/wood/tile/other

Yes   No

____ ____   1. Are interior walls in good shape (no major defects)?

____ ____   2. Are wallboard or plaster walls free of cracks?

____ ____   3. If no, are these cracks smaller than 1/4-inch wide? (Cracks 1/4-inch wide or larger may indicate structural failure.)

____ ____   4. Are walls straight (no unsightly bows)?

____ ____   5. Is all wallboard secured?

____ ____   6. Are plaster walls in good shape?

____ ____   7. Are the walls free of holes?

____ ____   8. Are all wood panels solidly attached and in good shape?

____ ____   9. Are walls free of leaks? (Check for water stains.)

____ ____   10. Does all wallpaper appear in good condition? (That is, it is not curled at the edges or faded.)

____ ____   11. Are ceilings free of cracks?

____ ____   12. If no, are these cracks smaller than 1/4-inch wide? (Larger ones may indicate structural failure.)

___ ___   13. Are all ceilings free of leaks (water stains)?

___ ___   14. Are walls and ceilings in good condition (no peeling paint or faded colors)?

___ ___   15. Are the plaster ceilings in good condition (no bubbles or raised portions)?

___ ___   16. Are all ceiling tiles in good shape?

___ ___   17. Push back suspended ceiling panels to examine hidden areas. Are they in good shape (no signs of deterioration in ceilings or walls)?

Trim

___ ___   18. Are the decorative moldings in good condition?

___ ___   19. Is the paint or stain on the trim in good shape (no peeling paint, no faded colors)?

Overall Rating   Good Fair Poor

Interior walls   ___   ___   ___
Ceilings   ___   ___   ___
Trim   ___   ___   ___
Major Problems:

Commonly Asked Questions

Q. Is hardboard paneling made from real wood?

A. Yes. Although hardboard is a manufactured product, it is an all-wood panel made from regular logs that have been converted to chips, then to wood fibers. The fibers are bonded together into sheets under heat and pressure.

Q. What kind of lumber is most solid wood paneling made from?

A. Although solid wood paneling can be made from any kind or grade of hardwood or softwood lumber, most is manufactured from western pine lumber.

Q. What is wainscotting?

A. Wainscotting is when the lower part of a wall is finished differently from the wall above. For example, ceramic tile is often used on the walls of baths in the form of wainscotting.

CHAPTER 14

Identifying Energy-Saving Features

Do memories of wintry chills penetrating your home still leave you cold? Regardless of how you answer, you should be aware of a variety of indoor and outdoor techniques and equipment that can make your home more snug, more energy efficient and more affordable to heat and cool.

Air Infiltration

In many older homes, and even some newer ones, a significant amount of heat loss in winter (or heat gain in summer) occurs around windows, doors and through a variety of little cracks, holes and spaces in a house's structure. In fact, it is estimated that windows and doors alone can account for as much as 25 percent of the total heat loss in a home.

Look for other air leaks through openings where plumbing or electrical wiring goes through walls, floors and ceilings. Check for drafts from electrical outlets, around ceiling fixtures and at openings in the attic. Seal cracks or holes.

Air leaks can also damage the house's insulation, because warm, moist air leaving the house dampens the insulation and reduces its heat-resisting effectiveness. And, of course, all that cold air entering the house means you have to raise the thermostat setting in order to keep warm. This forces the furnace to work harder and use more fuel to keep indoor air at a comfortable level. In the summer this works in reverse: unwanted hot air enters and welcome cool air escapes.

Caulking and Weatherstripping

The incidence of heat loss can be dramatically reduced by caulking and/or weatherstripping cracks and gaps around doors and windows. This can cut energy costs by as much as 10 percent a year.

Caulking is the process of applying a flexible, adhesive substance that is dispensed out of a cartridge by a special caulking gun. It is an inexpensive yet highly effective method of improving a home's energy efficiency.

Weatherstripping is a narrow piece of metal, vinyl, rubber, felt or foam that seals the contact area between the fixed and movable sections of a joint. Weatherstripping prevents air infiltration around windows and doors by eliminating gaps between the frames and the moving parts when they are closed. All exterior doors, as well as doors leading to an attic or garage, should be weatherized, as should all operable windows.

As a general rule, caulking and/or weatherstripping should be done anywhere that two different building materials meet. Some of the areas where heat loss or gain commonly occurs include around window and door frames where trim and siding meet, between foundation and siding, around air conditioners, around dryer vents, around pipe entries and under eaves (see Figure 14.1).

☞ **Money-$aving Tip #45** *If every gas-heated home were properly caulked and weatherstripped, we'd save enough natural gas each year to heat about 4 million homes.*

Energy-Saving Landscape

Although much attention is focused on constructing an energy-efficient home, sometimes little thought is given to the fact that proper landscaping can help reduce a home's energy consumption. Knowing a home's solar orientation and the direction of prevailing seasonal winds are critical starting points to a successful design.

The landscaping in Figure 14.2 is designed to battle the weather when it most threatens the home's heating and cooling bills. The shrubs on the property's north and west sides will take the bite out of those winter winds, while the deciduous shade trees will keep the house cool when the morning sun rises in the summer.

☞ **Money-$aving Tip #46** *Plant deciduous trees, shrubs and vines on south and west sides of the home to provide shade in the summer and sunshine in the winter.*

FIGURE 14.1 Where To Caulk and/or Weatherstrip

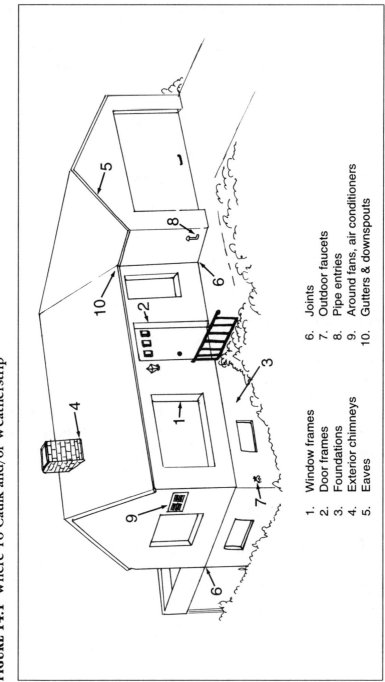

1. Window frames
2. Door frames
3. Foundations
4. Exterior chimneys
5. Eaves
6. Joints
7. Outdoor faucets
8. Pipe entries
9. Around fans, air conditioners
10. Gutters & downspouts

FIGURE 14.2 Energy-Saving Landscaping

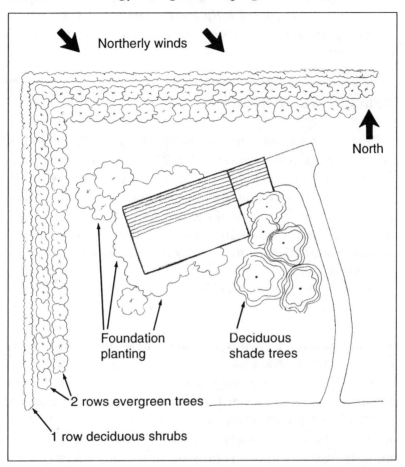

High-Efficiency Air Conditioners

There have been many significant improvements in the design of central air conditioners. A high-efficiency model can cut your air-conditioning cost in half, as well as greatly improve your family's comfort with much better control over air circulation. A high-efficiency air conditioner can also reduce the noise level both inside and outside your home.

☞ **Money-$aving Tip #47** *An energy-efficient appliance may cost more initially, but that expense is more than made up by reduced operating costs over the life of the appliance.*

Demand Water Heaters

One way to save on hot water bills is to use demand-type water heaters. A conventional hot water system heats water in a tank to a specified temperature. As heat is lost from the tank, the water is reheated until it reaches the specified temperature again. For most of the day, the water in the tank is not used, but it loses heat continually. Demand water heaters eliminate this problem by heating water only as hot water is drawn.

Demand water heaters, which use either gas or electricity, are rated according to the number of gallons of water per minute that can be raised a certain number of degrees in temperature. Typically, gas units heat more gallons per minute than electric units.

A demand water heater usually cannot provide large amounts of hot water at the same rate as a conventional water heater. For example, it could not provide 130°F water if the washer, shower and dishwasher are running simultaneously. It can, however, provide all the hot water needed if those appliances are used in succession.

☞ **Money-$aving Tip #48** *Heating water accounts for 15 to 25 percent of the average household energy budget.*

FIGURE 14.3 Turbine Attic Fans Can Reduce Air-Conditioning
Costs

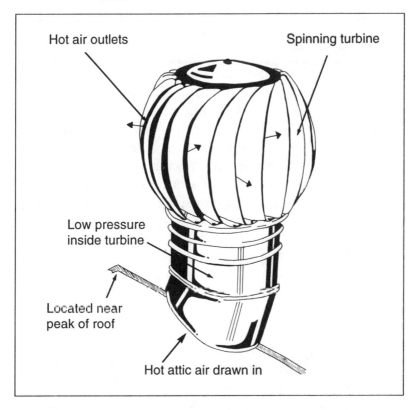

Turbine Attic Fans

Turbine attic vents (see Figure 14.3) can be extremely effective and energy efficient because they use no electricity. The wind blowing past the turbine causes it to spin.

By properly ventilating your attic, you can lower its peak temperature by 40 to 50 degrees. This not only reduces your air-conditioning costs and makes you more comfortable, but it increases the life of the roofing materials and structural lumber in your attic.

A great advantage of turbine vents is that they spin with the wind blowing from any direction. This is important because the prevailing wind direction changes from spring through fall and from day to day.

The centrifugal action of the spinning turbine blades creates an area of low pressure in its center. This low pressure area, along with the natural tendency of hot air to rise, draws the hot air out of your attic.

Turbine vents (generally more than one is needed) should be located as near as possible to the peak of the roof. This allows them to catch the wind from all directions without interference from the roof. The attic air is also hottest at the roof peak. It is also important to space them properly along the roof for effective ventilation.

☞ **Money-$aving Tip #49** *Eliminating heat loss will not only save you money now, but may add value to your home when it comes time to sell.*

How the Agent Can Help

Many utility companies offer low-cost or free home energy audits to identify areas where your home could be wasting energy and costing you money. If you're concerned about energy efficiency, ask your agent to arrange for a home energy audit.

Inspection Checklist

Yes   No

___   ___   1. Has an energy audit been done on the house?

___   ___   If so, were the results positive?

2. Does the house have sufficient insulation in

___   ___   ceilings?

___   ___   floors?

___   ___   walls?

___   ___   basement?

___   ___   3. Do the insulation materials have vapor barriers?

___   ___   4. Is all ductwork tightly sealed and insulated?

___   ___   5. Are water pipes insulated?

___   ___   6. Is there sufficient ventilation in the attic and crawl space?

___   ___   7. Does the house have an attic fan?

___   ___   8. Are all windows tight and free from air leaks?

___   ___   9. Do the windows have double-pane glass?

___   ___   10. Are all exterior doors tight fitting?

___   ___   11. Does the house have storm windows?

___   ___   12. Does the house have storm doors?

____ ____ 13. Is the house free of any significant air-infiltration problems?

____ ____ 14. Does the house have a high-efficiency heating and cooling system?

____ ____ 15. Is the heating and cooling unit properly sized for the number of square feet in the house?

____ ____ 16. Is the heating and cooling system in good working order?

____ ____ 17. Is the outside portion of the air conditioner in a shady location with free air circulation around it?

____ ____ 18. Does the fireplace have a high-quality, tight-fitting damper?

____ ____ 19. Does the fireplace have a glass front?

____ ____ 20. Are there deciduous trees and bushes on the south and west sides of the house to provide shade against the summer sun?

____ ____ 21. Are there evergreen trees and bushes on the north side of the house to act as a break against winter winds?

____ ____ 22. Are there ceiling fans throughout the house?

____ ____ 23. Check with the owners about the energy bills during the past year. Do they seem reasonable?

Overall Rating   **Good   Fair   Poor**

Total energy efficiency rating   ____   ____   ____
Major Problems:

Commonly Asked Questions

Q. What are the most frequent causes of discomfort and high energy bills?

A. The biggest culprits leading to discomfort and high energy bills are inadequate insulation, dirty furnace filters and air conditioner coils, faulty thermostats and leaky ducts.

Q. What percent of residential energy costs goes into heating and cooling our homes?

A. About 50 percent.

Q. When you use air-conditioning, what is recommended as a reasonably comfortable and energy-efficient indoor temperature?

A. 78°F. The higher the setting and the less difference between indoor and outdoor temperatures, the less outdoor hot air will flow into the building.

Q. What percent of the electricity used in homes goes into lighting?

A. About 15 percent. Most Americans overlight their homes, so lowering lighting levels is an easy energy conservation measure.

Q. What is a clock thermostat?

A. A clock thermostat does something most people forget to do. It turns the heat down for you automatically when you leave the house or go to bed, and turns it up again when you return or awaken.

CHAPTER 15

Testing for Environmental Hazards

Walk through the front door of a house and what do you see? Most likely, a cozy living or family room, fresh carpeting on the floor, painted walls, maybe even a fireplace.

It's hard to see any hazards to your health here, right? Well, take a deep breath. A main health threat inside a home is not anything you can see with the naked eye; it's the very air you breathe.

Gases from air fresheners, disinfectants and even carpeting can be harmful. So can dust from lead-based paint, mold spores from room humidifiers and air conditioners and fumes from scouring powders. The list goes on and on.

Some of these environmental hazards can have an immediate effect on our health. Others have long-term effects; scientists don't yet know the extent to which chronic exposure to low levels of pollutants will affect us.

We'll touch on just a few of these home hazards here.

Asbestos

Asbestos may be present in many materials in a home. Some materials where asbestos may be present in a home are in attic, wall, pipe or heating duct insulation; textured paint; wall patching compounds (spackling); roofing materials; floor tile; wood-burning fireplace and stove door gaskets; and some kitchen and laundry appliances.

Asbestos becomes a hazard when the materials are deteriorating or they are disturbed when making improvements. When you inhale the tiny airborne asbestos fibers, they become lodged in your lung tissues. They are suspected of causing lung cancer up to decades after you inhaled them. Asbestos exposure may also cause digestive tract and other cancers.

In most cases, asbestos-containing materials should be left alone. For example, undisturbed pipe or duct insulation that is in good condition does not release many asbestos fibers into the air.

Homeowners who suspect they have asbestos should hire trained and accredited asbestos inspectors who will have the asbestos tested at approved laboratories. It is not a job that homeowners should tackle themselves.

If you are concerned about a particular material in a home you're considering buying, a person experienced with asbestos (e.g., a plumber, building or heating contractor) can often make a reasonable judgment about whether it may contain asbestos. You can also have samples professionally tested for asbestos.

In any case, if you find asbestos-containing materials, **do not** try to remove them yourself. Have them professionally removed. Your regional Environmental Protection Agency (EPA) office can advise you about selecting a professional.

Formaldehyde

This chemical is found in urea formaldehyde foam insulation, particle board, hardwood plywood, furniture, cabinets and some synthetic carpeting and upholstery.

Inhaling vapors from formaldehyde-releasing materials may cause eye, nose, throat and skin irritation, headaches and dizziness. It is also a suspected human carcinogen.

Consider replacing the sources of such vapors with natural fiber carpeting and natural wood furniture. In addition, increase the room's ventilation and lower the temperature.

If you suspect a house has either urea formaldehyde foam insulation or asbestos insulation, bring in a qualified inspector to examine all questionable areas. It would probably be in your best interest to avoid homes with these kinds of insulation.

Fiberglass Insulation

Working with fiberglass insulation releases tiny particles of the material that can be inhaled. Scientists believe fiberglass may pose some of the same health risks as asbestos.

Be sure to wear a face mask when working with fiberglass. Keep children away from the areas where fiberglass is being handled and vacuum when finished.

Bacteria, Fungi and Molds

These biological agents live in air ducts, carpeting, air-conditioning and heating units and humidifiers. They can cause disease, allergic reactions and respiratory illness.

To protect yourself, keep the house as moisture-free as possible and keep susceptible appliances clean. Also, regularly inspect the ventilation system for cracks and breaks.

Combustion Gases

Improperly vented gas heaters, stoves and water heaters, wood-burning fireplaces and kerosene space heaters give off carbon monoxide and nitrogen dioxide (both of which are toxic), and sulfur dioxide, which can cause respiratory problems.

Wood-burning stoves and fireplaces give off creosote, which builds up in chimneys and creates a fire hazard.

Be sure to vent all fuel-burning devices to the outside and to have appliances serviced every year. If you burn wood in the fireplace, clean the chimney and flue yearly.

Lead Paint

Chances are, any home that was painted or remodeled before 1979 contains lead-based interior paint. This adds up to an estimated 57 million American homes.

Remodeling releases lead dust and chips into the air, putting children at most serious risk. Have the home tested for lead. If results are positive, hire a licensed contractor to remove it.

☞ **Money-$aving Tip #50** *Asbestos, formaldehyde and lead are indoor air contaminants that can lead to a variety of health problems—including an increased risk of cancer.*

FIGURE 15.1 Radon Entry Routes

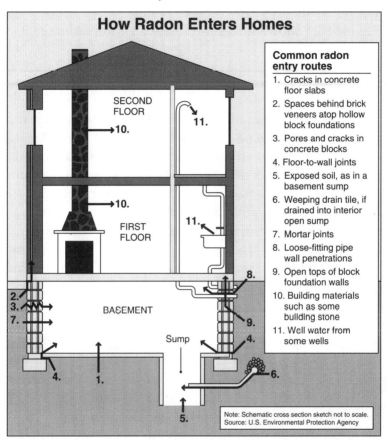

How Radon Enters Homes

SECOND
FLOOR

→10.

11.

→10.

FIRST
FLOOR

11.

8.

BASEMENT

2.
3.
7.

9.

Sump

4.

4.

1.

5.

6.

Common radon entry routes

1. Cracks in concrete floor slabs
2. Spaces behind brick veneers atop hollow block foundations
3. Pores and cracks in concrete blocks
4. Floor-to-wall joints
5. Exposed soil, as in a basement sump
6. Weeping drain tile, if drained into interior open sump
7. Mortar joints
8. Loose-fitting pipe wall penetrations
9. Open tops of block foundation walls
10. Building materials such as some building stone
11. Well water from some wells

Note: Schematic cross section sketch not to scale.
Source: U.S. Environmental Protection Agency

Radon

Radon is an odorless, colorless and tasteless gas caused by the radioactive decay of uranium and radium in rocks, water and soil. The gas seeps from the ground into houses. When breathed over long periods of time, risk of lung cancer increases.

Besides the most immediate concern about radon—the threat of cancer—homeowners also are worried about the impact of high radon levels on the value of real estate. As a result, many lenders now require radon testing.

Figure 15.1 shows how radon gas can enter a home.

Water Quality

We've all heard that our water isn't fit to drink, even if it looks and smells fine and comes to our taps after chlorination, fluoridation and all those other processes that supposedly make it pure. According to the EPA, every state's water supply is polluted. Lead, asbestos and toxic chemicals are just some of the contaminants that might enter the water in your house. Finding out if your water contains contaminants will require testing. Once you learn what, if any, contaminants need to be removed, you can then shop for the appropriate purifier.

How the Agent Can Help

Although most real estate agents do not have the training to recognize and assess environmental hazards, they should have information about the history of the neighborhood and potential environmental hazards in the area. A good agent will also study the seller's disclosure statement—if one is required in the state in which the property is located—to find out about the environmental condition of the property you are interested in.

If you're still not convinced, your agent can direct you to a specialist who is qualified to make an environmental assessment of the property.

☞ **Money-$aving Tip #51** *Ask the agent or seller if there have been any recent problems with water quality or supply.*

Inspection Checklist

Yes   No

——   ——   1. Is the property free of nearby environmental hazards (e.g., excessive noise, outdoor air pollution, underground storage tanks, etc.)?

2. Is the house free of

——   ——   radon gas (unsafe levels)?

——   ——   asbestos insulation?

urea formaldehyde insulation?

——   ——   lead pipes?

——   ——   lead paint?

——   ——   3. Is the water safe to drink?

Overall Rating   **Good   Fair   Poor**

Nearby environmental hazards   ——   ——   ——
Contaminants inside the home   ——   ——   ——
Major Problems:

Commonly Asked Questions

Q. *Where can I learn more about water purification?*

A. Contact the U.S. Environmental Protection Agency, Office of Drinking Water Criteria and Standards, in Washington, DC.

Q. *As a homeowner, can I legally remove asbestos-containing materials?*

A. You will need to check with the health or environmental agency that is responsible for asbestos programs in your area to determine if you are allowed to remove the material, whether a permit is needed, whether any regulations might apply and if there are special disposal requirements. Keep in mind that even if it is legal, removing asbestos from your house can be dangerous. The release of some asbestos fibers into the air cannot be avoided.

Q. *How can I tell if formaldehyde is a problem in my home?*

A. Formaldehyde irritates the eyes, nose and throat and causes nausea, coughing and other irritations if inhaled. The only sure way to know if you have a formaldehyde problem is to test for it. Check with your local or state department of health to find out if free or low-cost tests are available.

Q. *What is the most common source of lead exposure for children?*

A. Lead-based paint. Before 1950, paint that contained high levels of lead was widely used. Although the use of lead-based paint decreased after 1950, it continued to be available until the mid-1970s. It was banned for use on interior and exterior residential surfaces in 1978.

Q. What steps can be taken immediately to lower the radon level in a house?

A. Opening windows, doors and vents usually can decrease indoor radon levels.

```
┌─────────────────────────┐
│  ┌───────────────────┐  │
│  │                   │  │
│  │  C H A P T E R  1 6 │  │
│  │                   │  │
│  └───────────────────┘  │
└─────────────────────────┘
```

Using Today's Technology To Help

Whether it's a notebook or a desktop model, computers have become an integral tool for real estate brokers and agents. Computers can save agents time by calculating complex financing deals or sifting through vast databases to find a handful of homes for a potential buyer.

Many agents use personal computers connected to a mainframe computer at their local Board of REALTORS®. The computer maintains all active property listings and sales information, including homes, condominiums, commercial properties and vacant land. It also sends updates on this data to each office in the network and gives agents a chance to exchange messages.

In addition to reducing the time it takes to do complex figuring, computers also reduce the chance for human error.

Computer Terminology

To understand the impact of computers on the real estate industry, you should be familiar with certain terms.

Cyberspace. The imaginary place where people communicate and view text and pictures using their personal computers.

Internet. A worldwide community of people using computers to interact. It is a way to get information on a variety of topics.

Modem. A device that translates digitized computer information into signals that can be transmitted over telephone lines.

World Wide Web. An internet tool that allows viewing pages that can include text, photographs and sound.

Home page. A World Wide Webb page that serves to introduce an organization or individual to other users. By clicking on underlined words in the home page, users can see related pages.

Online. Using computers to access information from other computers via telephone lines and modems.

Cyberspace

The Internet's World Wide Web is the newest of many tools real estate companies use to market properties.

The open house remains an effective way for real estate brokers and agents to publicize both homes for sale and themselves. It provides the broker or agent with the opportunity to show the property and to discuss its features. Most importantly, however, the broker or agent can gather input from prospective buyers. What's new as we approach the 21st century is that many brokers and agents are holding an open house without setting foot on the property. Instead, many are putting their listings—and information about their companies—on the World Wide Webb, where they're holding "virtual" open houses. There, prospective buyers across the world can view neighborhoods and homes via personal computers and modems. They can see street maps, property tax figures, and other public information and census data for any particular area that interests them.

With a few keystrokes, it's possible to view photos and text describing a $5 million estate in England or a charming little house in North Carolina for under $100,000.

How the Agent Can Help

More and more real estate offices can guide you through the Internet's World Wide Webb to assist with your house-hunting. As great as it is to sit at home or at a broker's office and look at houses on a computer screen, it's highly unlikely you or anyone else is going to buy a home without leaving cyberspace and visiting real space.

While brokers and agents have embraced pagers, cellular phones and computers, buying and selling real estate is still a person-to-person interaction. The key to finding a house—as always—is a broker or agent who knows the market and will work seven days a week to help you. And, a computer will never replace personal service.

Inspection Tools and Gear

In order to conduct a home inspection, you will need the following:

1. A flashlight for checking in dark corners of basements, crawl spaces and attics
2. A probing tool, such as a screwdriver, to check for signs of wood decay or structural pest damage
3. Binoculars for looking at the roof and chimney from the ground; or an extension ladder if you'd prefer to climb up on the roof
4. A sturdy stepladder to use in those houses that do not provide direct access to the attic
5. An electrical tester to check outlets
6. A marble or level to determine if the floors are level (the level can also be used to check if the walls are plumb)
7. A tape measure to measure rooms and other spaces in the house
8. A clipboard, pen or pencils, and some ruled graph paper to draw an accurate floor plan for you to study
9. A compass to determine the house's climatic exposure
10. The inspection checklists provided in this book
11. Old clothes, work gloves and shoes with nonskid soles and good supports

Cutaway View of a Typical House with Areas To Check

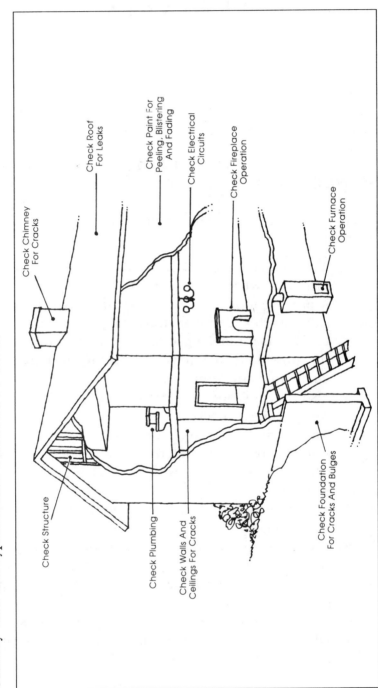

Check Chimney For Cracks

Check Roof For Leaks

Check Paint For Peeling, Blistering And Fading

Check Electrical Circuits

Check Fireplace Operation

Check Furnace Operation

Check Structure

Check Plumbing

Check Walls And Ceilings For Cracks

Check Foundation For Cracks And Bulges

House Diagram

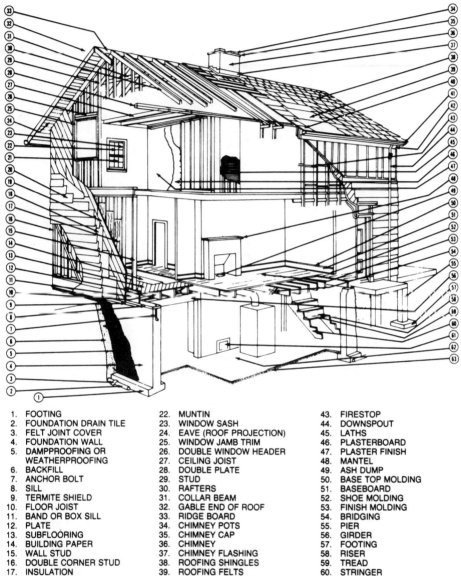

1. FOOTING	22. MUNTIN	43. FIRESTOP
2. FOUNDATION DRAIN TILE	23. WINDOW SASH	44. DOWNSPOUT
3. FELT JOINT COVER	24. EAVE (ROOF PROJECTION)	45. LATHS
4. FOUNDATION WALL	25. WINDOW JAMB TRIM	46. PLASTERBOARD
5. DAMPPROOFING OR	26. DOUBLE WINDOW HEADER	47. PLASTER FINISH
WEATHERPROOFING	27. CEILING JOIST	48. MANTEL
6. BACKFILL	28. DOUBLE PLATE	49. ASH DUMP
7. ANCHOR BOLT	29. STUD	50. BASE TOP MOLDING
8. SILL	30. RAFTERS	51. BASEBOARD
9. TERMITE SHIELD	31. COLLAR BEAM	52. SHOE MOLDING
10. FLOOR JOIST	32. GABLE END OF ROOF	53. FINISH MOLDING
11. BAND OR BOX SILL	33. RIDGE BOARD	54. BRIDGING
12. PLATE	34. CHIMNEY POTS	55. PIER
13. SUBFLOORING	35. CHIMNEY CAP	56. GIRDER
14. BUILDING PAPER	36. CHIMNEY	57. FOOTING
15. WALL STUD	37. CHIMNEY FLASHING	58. RISER
16. DOUBLE CORNER STUD	38. ROOFING SHINGLES	59. TREAD
17. INSULATION	39. ROOFING FELTS	60. STRINGER
18. BUILDING PAPER	40. ROOF SHEATHING	61. CLEANOUT DOOR
19. WALL SHEATHING	41. EAVE TROUGH OR GUTTER	62. CONCRETE BASEMENT FLOOR
20. SIDING	42. FRIEZE BOARD	63. CINDER FILL
21. MULLION		

GLOSSARY

access The right to enter and leave a tract of land from a public way, sometimes by easement over land owned by another.

acoustical material Sound-absorbing materials, such as tile or fiberboard, which are applied to walls and/or ceilings.

acoustical tile Tile, usually made of mineral, fiber or insulated metal material, having the inherent property of sound absorption.

airway A space between roof insulation and roof boards for movement of air.

anchor bolt A bolt that secures the sill of the house to the foundation wall.

asphalt tile A resilient floor covering laid in mastic (a thick adhesive).

attic ventilators Openings in the roof or in gables to allow for air circulation.

backfill The earth or gravel used to fill in the space around a building wall after the foundation is completed.

balloon framing A type of framing in which the studs extend from the top of the foundation sill to the roof. Support for the second floor is provided by a horizontal ribbon or ledge board and by joists that are nailed to the studs.

baseboard A board running along the bottom of the wall parallel to the floor. A baseboard covers the gap between the floor and the wall, protects the wall from scuffs and provides a decorative accent.

baseboard heating A system of perimeter heating with radiators, convectors or air outlets located in the wall. The system may be hot water, forced air or electric.

basement A space of full-story height below the first floor, wholly or partly below the exterior grade, which is not used primarily for living accommodations. Space partly below grade that is used primarily for living accommodations or commercial use is not defined by FHA as basement space.

179

base shoe Molding used at the junction of the baseboard and the floor. Also called a **carpet strip**.

batten Narrow decorative strips of wood or metal used to cover interior or exterior joints.

bay window A window that forms a bay in a room, projects outward from the wall and is supported by its own foundation.

beam A structural member that transversely supports a load.

beamed ceiling A ceiling with beams exposed.

bearing plate A metal plate placed under a column or beam to distribute the weight of the load.

bearing wall A wall that supports any vertical load in addition to its own weight.

bevel An angular surface across an edge of a piece of stock.

blacktop Bituminous or asphalt material used in hard surface paving.

blueprint (1) A working plan used on a construction job by tradespeople. (2) An architectural drafting or drawing that is transferred to chemically treated paper by exposure to strong light that turns the paper blue, thus reproducing the drawing in white.

board and batten A type of vertical siding composed of wide boards and narrow battens. The boards are nailed to the sheathing with a one-half space left between them. The battens are then nailed over the spaces.

board foot A measure of lumber one foot square by one inch thick; 144 cubic inches = 1 foot by 1 foot by 1 inch.

bracing Framing lumber nailed at an angle to provide rigidity.

brick veneer A facing of brick laid against and fastened to the sheathing of a frame wall.

bridging Small wood or metal pieces placed diagonally between the floor joists. Bridgings disburse weight on the floor over adjacent joists, thus increasing the floor's load capacity.

BTU British thermal unit. One BTU is the amount of heat required to raise one pound of water 1 degree Fahrenheit.

built-up roof A roof composed of three to five layers of asphalt felt laminated with coal tar, pitch or asphalt, and coated with gravel. Generally used on flat or low-pitched roofs.

BX Electrical cable consisting of a flexible metal covering enclosing two or more wires.

casement window A type of window having a sash with hinges on the side and opening outward.

casing A frame, as of a window or door.

ceiling joists The horizontal structural members to which the ceiling is fastened.

cement blocks Blocks made primarily of cement and gravel formed into shape under pressure and used principally for construction of walls.

cesspool A covered cistern of stone, brick or concrete block that functions like a septic tank. The liquid seeps out through the walls directly into the surrounding earth.

chimney A stack of brick or other masonry extending above the surface of the roof that carries the smoke to the outside. The smoke is carried inside the chimney through the flue.

chimney cap Ornamental stone or concrete edging around the top of the chimney stack that helps protect the masonry from the elements and improves the draft in the chimney.

chimney flashing A strip of material, usually metal, placed over the junction of the chimney and the roof to make the joint watertight. Flashings are used wherever the slope is broken up by a vertical structure.

chimney pot A fire clay or terra-cotta pipe projecting from the top of the chimney stack. The chimney pot is decorative and increases the draft of the chimney.

cinder fill A layer of cinder placed between the ground and the basement floor or between the ground and the foundation walls to aid in water drainage.

clapboard Siding of narrow boards thicker at one edge used as exterior finish for frame houses.

collar beam A horizontal beam connecting the rafter at the lower end. The collar beam adds rigidity and diverts the weight of snow on the roof from the exterior walls.

collector A device use to collect solar radiation and convert it into heat.

column A vertical structural member supporting horizontal members such as beams and girders.

concrete A combination of cement and sand, broken stone or gravel used for foundations, walks and other construction purposes.

concrete block Concrete compressed into the shape of a block and allowed to set until it hardens; used as a masonry unit.

conduit A metal pipe in which electrical wire is installed.

cornice (1) A horizontal projection or molding at the top of the exterior walls under the eaves that aids in water drainage. (2) Any molded projection at the top of an interior or exterior wall, in the enclosure at the roof eaves, or at the inclined edge of a gable roof.

cove molding A molding with a concave face used as trim or as a finish around interior corners.

crawl space A shallow space between the floor of a house and the ground.

crown molding Molding that is installed between the top of the wall and the ceiling.

damper An adjustable valve at the top of a fireplace that regulates the flow of heated gases into the chimney.

dampproofing or weatherproofing A horizontal layer of plastic, asphalt or other water-resistant materials placed between the interior and exterior walls to keep out moisture.

deciduous trees Trees that lose their leaves annually.

design An architectural drawing of the plan, elevations and sections of a structure.

DOE Department of Energy.

dormer A projection built out from the slope of a roof, used to house windows on the upper floor and to provide additional headroom. Common types of dormers are the gable dormer and the shed dormer.

double floor Wood construction using a subfloor and a finished floor.

double-hung window A type of window containing two movable sashes that slide vertically.

double pitch Sloping in two directions, as in a gable roof.

downspout A vertical pipe made of cement, metal, clay or plastic that carries rainwater from the eaves to the ground.

drain field An area containing a system of underground pipes for draining septic systems or other types of liquid overflow.

drain tile A pipe, usually clay, placed next to the foundation footing to aid in water drainage.

dry rot Decay of seasoned wood caused by a fungus.

drywall construction Any type of interior wall construction not using plaster as finish material. Wood paneling, plywood, plasterboard, gypsum board or other types of wallboard are usually used for drywall.

duct A tube, pipe or channel for conveying or carrying fluids, cables, wires or tempered air.

dutch door A door divided horizontally so that the top half may be opened while the lower section remains closed.

eave The overhang of a sloping roof that extends beyond the walls of the house. Also called roof projection.

EPA Environmental Protection Agency.

exterior finish The outer finish of a structure including roof and wall covering, gutters and door and window frames. The term generally refers to the protective outer coating of a structure.

exterior wall Any outer wall serving as the vertical enclosure of a building.

facade The principal exterior face of a structure; usually the front face or front elevation of a building.

face The most important side of a structure; the front or facade.

face brick A better grade of brick that is used on the exterior wall of a building, frequently only on the front or principal side.

fascia The board of the cornice to which the gutter for rainwater is fastened.

felt paper Paper used for sheathing on walls and roofs to serve as a barrier against heat, cold and moisture.

fenestration The arrangement and design of doors and windows in a wall.

FHA Federal Housing Administration.

fiberboard A prefabricated building material composed of wood or other plant fibers, compressed and bonded into a sheet.

finish flooring The visible interior floor surface, which is usually made of a decorative hardwood such as oak. The finish flooring may be laid in strips or in a block design such as parquet.

fire brick A clay brick capable of resisting high temperatures; it is used to line heating chambers and fireplaces.

firestop Short boards placed horizontally between studs or joists to decrease drafts and retard fires.

fire wall A wall constructed of fire-resistant materials, the purpose of which is to prevent the spread of fire within the building. The fire wall carries a standard rating that designates its ability to constrain fire in terms of hours.

fixed window A window that does not open, such as a picture window.

flashing Sheet metal or other impervious material used in roof and wall construction to protect a building from water seepage.

flat roof A roof having a slope sufficient to provide for proper drainage.

floor joists Horizontal boards laid on edge resting on the beams that provide the main support for the floor. The subflooring is nailed directly to the joists.

flue An enclosed passage in a chimney, duct or pipe through which smoke, hot air and gases pass upward. Flues are usually made of fire clay or terra-cotta pipe.

footing A concrete support under a foundation, chimney or column that usually rests on solid ground and is wider than the structure being supported. Footings are designed to distribute the weight of the structure over the ground.

Formica A trade name for a plastic material that is used primarily for the top of counter areas, but is also used for wall covering, as a veneer for plywood panels or as a wallboard where a fire-resistant material is desirable.

foundation The part of a building or wall that supports the **superstructure.**

foundation wall The **masonry** or **concrete** wall below ground level that serves as the main support for the frame structure. Foundation walls form the side walls of the basement.

frame construction Construction in which the structural parts are of wood or depend on a wood frame for support.

framing The rough structure of a building, including interior and exterior walls, floor, roof and ceiling.

french windows or doors A pair of glazed doors hinged at the jamb, functioning as both windows and doors.

frieze A horizontal member of a cornice, set flat against a wall.

frost line The depth of frost penetration in the soil. The frost line varies throughout the United States, and footings should be placed below this depth to prevent movement of the structure.

furring strips Narrow strips of wood nailed or glued on walls and ceilings to form a level surface on which to fasten other materials.

gable (1) The end of a building, generally triangular in shape. (2) The vertical plane that lies above the eaves and between the slopes of a ridged roof.

gable roof A ridged roof, the ends of which form a gable.

gambrel roof A variation of the gable roof, having a steep lower slope and a flatter one above, as seen in Dutch Colonial architecture.

girder A heavy wooden or steel beam supporting the floor joists. The girder provides the main horizontal support for the floor.

green lumber Freshly sawed lumber, or lumber that has had no intentional drying; unseasoned.

grout A cement mixture used to fill crevices.

gutter A shallow metal channel set below and along the eaves of a house to catch and carry off rainwater from the roof.

hardwood Refers not to the hardness of the wood, but to a group of broadleafed trees from which the wood is taken. Maple, oak and birch are hardwood trees. See **softwood**.

head casing The strip of molding placed above a door or window frame.

head jamb A piece of finish material across the underside of the top of a door or window opening.

hearth The floor of the fireplace. The front hearth, which extends out into the room, may be made of brick or decorative stone. The back hearth inside the fireplace is usually made of fire brick.

heating system Any device or system for heating a building; usually a furnace or boiler used to generate hot air, hot water or steam.

hip roof A pitched roof with sloping sides and ends.

insulation Pieces of plasterboard, fireproofed sheeting, compressed wood-wool, fiberboard or other material placed between inner and outer surfaces, such as walls and ceilings, to protect the interior from heat loss or heat gain. Insulation works by breaking up and dissipating air currents.

jalousie Adjustable glass louvers in doors and windows used to regulate light and air or keep out rain.

jamb A vertical surface lining the opening in the wall left for a door or window.

joint The point where two surfaces join or meet.

joist A heavy piece of horizontal timber to which the boards of a floor or the lath of a ceiling are nailed. Joists are nailed edgewise to form the floor support.

kick plate A metal strip placed at the lower edge of a door to protect the finish.

lath Thin strips of wood, metal or gypsum fastened to rafters, ceiling joists or wall studs to act as a plaster base.

lean-to roof A sloping roof supported on one side by the wall of an adjacent building.

linear measure Measurement along a line.

lintel A horizontal board that supports the load over an opening, such as a door or window.

load Weight supported by a structural part such as a load-bearing wall.

low E glass Glass used in dual-glazed windows. It has a low emissivity (low E) coating on the inside to reduce heat loss in the winter and heat gain in the summer.

mansard roof A roof with two slopes or pitches on each of the four sides, with the lower slope steeper than the upper.

mantel The decorative facing placed around a fireplace. Mantels are usually made of ornamental wood and topped by a shelf.

masonry Anything constructed of brick, stone, tile, cement, concrete or similar materials.

masonry wall A wall made of masonry materials. See **masonry**.

millwork Wooden parts of a building purchased in finished form from millwork plants and planing mills. Doors, window and door frames, trim, molding, stairways and cabinets are millwork items.

miter In carpentry terminology, the ends of two pieces of board of corresponding form cut off at an angle and fitted together in an angular shape.

molding A strip of decorative wood, such as that on the top of a baseboard or around windows and doors.

mud room A vestibule or small room used as the entrance from a play yard or alley. The mud room frequently contains a washer and dryer.

mullion A thin vertical bar or divider in the frame between windows, doors or other openings.

muntin The narrow vertical strip that separates two adjacent window sashes.

NEC National Electrical Code.

OC (on center) The measurement of spacing for studs, rafters, joists and similar members in a building from the center of one member to the center of the next.

orientation The position and direction of the house on the site.

overhang The part of a roof that extends beyond the exterior wall.

parquet floor A finished floor constructed of wood blocks laid in rectangular or square patterns.

partition That which subdivides space within a building—especially an interior wall.

pitch The slope or incline of a roof from the ridge to the lower edge, expressed in inches of rise per foot of length, or by the ratio of the rise to the span.

plank-and-beam framing A type of frame construction that uses heavier structural members spaced farther apart than other framing, and with the supporting posts, roof beams and roof deck left exposed to the interior as part of the decor.

plat A map representing a piece of land subdivided into lots, with streets and other details shown thereon.

plate A horizontal piece that forms a base for supports. The sill or sole plate rests on the foundation and forms the base for the studs. The wall plate is laid along the top of the wall studs and forms a support base for the rafters.

platform or western frame A type of framing in which floor joists of each story rest on the top plates of the story below (or on the foundation sill for the first story). The bearing walls and partitions rest on the subfloor of each story.

plumb Vertical.

ply A term to denote the number of layers or thicknesses of material, such as three-ply building or roofing paper.

plywood A wood product made of three or more (but always an odd number) layers of veneer joined with an adhesive and usually laid with the grain of adjoining plies at right angles.

prefabrication The manufacturing and assembling of construction materials and parts into component structural units such as floor, wall and roof panels, which are later erected or installed at the construction site.

purlin A horizontal structural member used to support roof rafters or roof sheathing.

quarter round A molding whose shape forms a quarter of a circle.

R-value A number indicating insulation performance. The higher the R-value, the greater the insulating effectiveness.

rafter One of a series of sloping beams that extends from the exterior wall to a center ridge board and provides the main support for the roof.

ranch house A one-story house that is low to the ground, with low-pitched gable roof or roofs. It may have a basement.

retaining wall Any wall erected to hold back or support a bank of earth. A retaining wall is also any wall built to resist the lateral pressure of internal loads.

ridge board A heavy horizontal board set on edge at the apex of the roof to which the rafters are attached.

roof boards Boards nailed to the top of the rafters, usually touching each other, to tie the roof together and form a base for the roofing material. The boards, or roof sheathing, can also be constructed of sheets of plywood.

roofing felt Sheets of felt or other close-woven heavy material placed on the top of the roof boards to insulate and waterproof the roof. Like building paper, roofing felt is treated with bitumen or another tar derivative to increase its water resistance. Roofing felt is applied either with a bonding and sealing compound or with intense heat that softens the tar and causes it to adhere to the roof.

roof sheathing The material, usually wood boards, plywood or wallboard, fastened to the roof rafters and onto which shingles or other roof coverings are laid.

saddle Two sloping surfaces meeting in a horizontal ridge, used between the back side of a chimney and a sloping roof.

sash The framework that holds the glass in a window or door.

scale A proportion between two sets of dimensions, such as between those of a drawing and the actual structure. The scale of a floor plan may be expressed as 1/4 inch = 1 foot. This means that one-quarter inch on the drawing is the same as one foot in the actual structure.

SEER Seasonal Energy Efficiency Ratio. SEER is a measure of central air conditioner efficiency.

sheathing Plywood or boards nailed to the studs and roof rafters on the exterior of a house as a foundation for the finished siding and roofing.

shingle A roof or wall covering material usually made of asphalt, wood, slate or tile, applied in overlapping layers.

shoe molding A thin strip of wood placed at the junction of the baseboard and the floor boards to conceal the joint. The shoe molding improves the aesthetics of the room and helps seal out drafts.

siding Boards, metal or masonry sheets nailed horizontally to the vertical studs, with or without intervening sheathing, to form the exposed surface of the outside walls of the house.

sill The lowest horizontal member of the house frame, which rests on the top of the foundation walls and forms a base for the studs. The term can also refer to the lowest horizontal member in a frame for a window or door.

slab A flat, horizontal reinforced concrete area, usually the interior floor of a building.

sleepers Strips of wood laid over rough concrete floors so a finished wood floor can be applied over them.

soffit Usually the underside of a roof overhang or eaves, frequently with openings for attic ventilation.

softwood A general classification of lumber obtained from the group of trees having needlelike leaves. The common softwoods are cedar, fir, pine, redwood and spruce. See **hardwood**.

solar heating A system that operates by gathering the heat from the sun's rays with one or more solar collectors. Water or air is forced through a series of pipes in the solar collector to be heated by the sun. The hot air or water is then stored in a heavily insulated tank until it is needed to heat the house.

span The horizontal distance between structural supports such as walls, beams, columns, girders and tresses.

split-level house A house in which two or more floors are usually located directly above one another and one or more additional floors, adjacent to them, are placed at a different level.

storm window An extra window usually placed on the outside of an existing window as additional protection against cold weather.

stucco A cement or plaster wallcovering that is installed wet and dries into a hard surface covering.

stud In wall framing, the vertical members to which horizontal pieces are attached. Studs are placed between 16 and 24 inches apart and serve as the main support for the roof and/or the second floor.

subfloor Boards or plywood sheets nailed directly to the floor joists serving as a base for the finish flooring. Subflooring is usually made of rough boards, although some houses have concrete subflooring.

sump A pit or reservoir used for collecting or holding water (or some other liquid) that is subsequently disposed of, usually by a pump.

sump pump An automatic electric pump installed in a basement or low area to empty the sump. See **sump**.

superstructure That part of the structure above the ground or above the top of the foundation walls.

suspended ceiling A ceiling system that derives its support from the overhead structural framing.

termite shield A metal sheet laid into the exterior walls of a house near ground level, usually under the sill, to prevent termites from entering the house. Termite shields should be affixed to all exterior wood in the house and around pipes entering the building. Shields are generally constructed with an overhanging lip to allow for water runoff.

tongue-and-groove A method of joining two pieces of board wherein one has a tongue cut into the edge and the other board has a groove cut to receive the corresponding tongue. The method is used to modify any material prepared for joining in this fashion, as tongue-and-groove lumber.

trim Wood or metal interior finishing pieces such as door and window casings, moldings and hardware.

truss A type of roof construction employing a rigid framework of beams and members, which supports the roof load and usually achieves relatively wide spans between its supports.

U-value The total number of BTUs of heat transmitted in one hour per square foot of area per 1° Fahrenheit difference between the air on one side of a barrier and the air on the other side.

valley The internal angle formed by the junction of two sloping sides of a roof.

vapor barrier Material used to keep moisture from penetrating walls or floors.

veneer (1) A layer of material covering a base of another substance, such as mahogany veneer overlaid on a less valuable wood. (2) A brick exterior finish over wood framing.

vent A small opening to allow the passage of air through any space in a building, as for ventilation of an attic or the unexcavated area under a first-floor construction.

vestibule A small entrance hall to a building or to a room.

wainscot Wainscotting is the lower part of a wall when finished differently from the wall above.

wallboard A board used as the finishing covering for an interior wall or ceiling. Wallboard can be made of plastic, laminated plywood, cement sheeting, plywood, molded gypsum, plasterboard or other materials. Wallboard is applied in thin sheets over the insulation. It is often used today as a substitute for plaster walls but can also serve as a base for plaster.

wall sheathing Sheets of plywood, gypsum board or other material nailed to the outside face of the wall studs to form a base for exterior siding.

warm-air system A heating system in which furnace-heated air moves to living space through a single register or a series of ducts, circulated by natural convection (gravity system) or by a fan or blower in the ductwork (forced system).

waste line A pipe that carries waste from a bathtub, shower, lavatory or any fixture or appliance except a toilet.

weatherstrip A thin strip of material, such as metal, felt or wood, used around doors and windows to keep out air, water, moisture or dust.

window sash A movable frame that holds the window glass. Sash windows move vertically and may be single, in which only the lower half of the window opens; or double, in which both the upper and lower portions are movable.

X-bracing Cross-bracing in a partition.

INDEX

A

Access to services, 13
Additions, 39
Agent assistance
  architecture and house style preferences, 42
  computer access, 173
  energy audits, 156
  environmental hazard information, 166
  floor plans, 52
  insulation, 110
  mechanical systems, 131
  moving needs, 8
  neighborhood evaluation, 18
  radon gas test, 67
  roofs, 80
  site selection, 27
  termite test, 67
Air-conditioning, 44, 107, 120-23
  environmental hazard of, 163-64
  heat pump, 121
  high-efficiency, 122, 153-54
  inspecting, 123-25
  room, 122-23
  Seasonal Energy Efficiency Ratio (SEER), 120
Air infiltration, 149-50
Allergic reactions, 163
Aluminum
  doors, 99

  roof material, 73
  siding, 86, 90, 91
  window frames, 98
American Society of Home Inspectors, 1
Amperage, 127
Architectural styles, 33-34, 35. *See also* House types
Asbestos, 162, 168
Asphalt flooring, 137
Asphalt roof shingles, 72-73, 83-84
Attic
  ceiling water stains, 75
  fans, 155-56
  insulation, 107, 108
  ventilation, 75, 155
  windows, 94
Awning windows, 94

B

Bacteria, 163-64
Basement, 51, 63-64
Bathroom(s), 38, 49-50
  fixtures, 114
  walls, 144, 145, 148
Bedrooms, 38, 49, 58
  master suite, 50
Brick veneer, 87-88, 91

193

ABOUT THE AUTHOR

Over the past 25 years, the CENTURY 21® name has held the distinction of being the undisputed leader in the real estate industry. We have helped millions of people through the exciting adventure of selling their home or finding the home of their dreams. In the relocation process as well, CENTURY 21® experts have been with families every step of the way.

To meet the high expectations of today's demanding, value-conscious consumer, the CENTURY 21® System now offers an array of home-related products and services, including CENTURY 21® Home Improvements, computer online listings and homebuyer information services, *CENTURY 21® House & Home* magazine and other housing-related services.

As America enters the 21st century, the nation's most professional, best-trained home ownership experts are at your service at each and every one of the CENTURY 21® System's 6,000 independently owned offices in all 50 states and throughout the world.

Find this book useful for your real estate needs?

Discover *all* the bestselling CENTURY 21® Guides.

CENTURY 21® Guide to Buying Your Home

CENTURY 21® Guide to Choosing Your Mortgage

CENTURY 21® Guide to Inspecting Your Home